EASY AND DELICIOUS PLANT-BASE

Using Exciting Ingredients—from Aquafaba to

THE
VEGAN
ABCs
COOKBOOK

LISA DAWN ANGERAME

Author of *Wait, That's Vegan?!*

Photography by Alexandra Shytsman

PAGE STREET
PUBLISHING CO.

PAGE STREET
PUBLISHING CO.

Distributed by Macmillan, sales in Canada by The Canadian Manda Group.

25 24 23 22 21   1 2 3 4 5

ISBN-13: 978-1-64567-265-4
ISBN-10: 1-64567-265-4

Library of Congress Control Number: 2020947782

Cover and book design by Meg Baskis for Page Street Publishing Co.
Photography by Alexandra Shytsman

Printed and bound in China

DEDICATION

For everyone who wants to learn how to make
easy and delicious vegan food!

INTRODUCTION

I've always loved being in the kitchen. My earliest food memory is of me standing on a little step stool helping my 90-year-old Russian great-grandmother make kreplach. Helping might not be that accurate—I was probably three or four years old—but I was there, where all of the action was, and I never left!

Growing up, I did my homework at the kitchen table, waiting for my mother to come home so we could make dinner together. I loved waking up on Sundays to help my father make his famous hash browns and eggs-in-a-hole. (It was my job to use a shot glass to make the hole.) We made all kinds of recipes, family favorites and holiday specials, bonding over eggplant Parmesan and potato pancakes and dry white wine and chocolate cake.

I went to college in Los Angeles, where I discovered California cuisine and new-to-me ingredients like avocados and artichokes and sourdough bread. After graduation, I moved back to New York, where I cooked for myself in my little galley kitchen, happily making old favorites and inventing new ones.

Eventually, I made the decision to go vegan after learning about how animals are raised for food, what animal agriculture does to the environment and how eating animals affects human health. I made myself one last bowl of shrimp scampi and said goodbye to animal products forever. But I woke up the next day and realized I had no idea what to do in the kitchen. Basically, I had to learn how to cook all over again.

And when I say learn how to cook all over again, it wasn't that I needed to learn how to cook. I knew how to sauté and steam and roast and boil and bake. I needed to figure out what to cook. For some reason, it didn't seem all that easy, so I just ate out a lot. Luckily, I live only nine blocks away from Candle Cafe, one of the best vegan restaurants in town. But, eventually, I was inspired to learn everything I could about vegan ingredients and how to cook them. I love a good project, so I picked up a couple of vegan cookbooks and took a plant-based nutrition course, a plant-based professional cooking course and an essential vegan baking course.

I researched and taste-tested and played around in the kitchen. It wasn't always pretty, but it sure was fun. I spent hours working out ways to elevate plants from side-dish status to the center of my plate. To make it happen, I filled my pantry and refrigerator with all kinds of ingredients that, just a few short years earlier, I literally didn't even know existed, using them to build flavor, inspired by cuisines from all over the world. I started making really delicious, satisfying and mouthwatering vegan meals in my own kitchen! How?

I added fresh herbs like parsley and chives to my weekly shopping list. I got a citrus zester and a garlic press. I bought some Aleppo pepper, which is kind of like a milder, fruity version of crushed red pepper and one of my favorite spices. (Get a jar—I promise you will love it too.)

I expanded my vinegar collection beyond balsamic and bought bottles of tamari, tubs of miso, bags of nutritional yeast and jars of umeboshi paste. If you just read that last sentence and you have no idea what I'm talking about, don't worry, by the time you get from A to Z you will!

In the pages that follow, you will find an alphabetical list of 26 star ingredients, a fun way to initiate you into the vast world of plant-based cooking. And when I say vast, I mean vast! Because, if you think about it, with the exception of meat and dairy, everything is already vegan, and that's a lot of food! Fruits and vegetables. Grains and greens. Legumes and beans.

So, I curated this list of ingredients not just because they are vegan but because they are awesome. Straight up fruits and vegetables like beets, dates, eggplant, kale, portobellos and zucchini. Whole grains like oats, quinoa, rice, barley, millet and buckwheat. Protein-rich ingredients like garbanzo beans and lentils. Flavor makers like coconut milk, herbs, miso, umeboshi and vinegar.

And then there are those ingredients that are more likely to be found in a vegan kitchen. Aquafaba, the coolest egg replacer since sliced bread. Jackfruit, the plant-based white meat. Nutritional yeast, a flaky seasoning that tastes like cheese. Tempeh and tofu, soy-based plant proteins. But I am here to tell you that once you understand what they are—and how to cook with them—they will soon have a place in your kitchen too!

Altogether, these ingredients make up a little universe, crisscrossing these pages, showing up in recipes as supporting actors even when they are not the star of the show, working together to bring out their potential for deliciousness. Because with a little imagination and creativity, every single one can be transformed into drool-worthy meals from flavorful, hearty soups and salads to plant-based tacos, omelets, lasagna, steak, cake and more!

As you cook your way from A to Z, you will find nutritional information, fun facts like why people think beets taste like dirt and how ancient foods like quinoa survived to become modern-day superfoods, nutritional information, how-tos and answers to your most frequently asked questions like "Where do you get your protein?"

In the end, you will be so familiar with each and every ingredient that you will be able to walk into your kitchen with confidence and whip up a tasty meal like a plant-based pro.

So, what are you waiting for? Get cooking!

Lisa

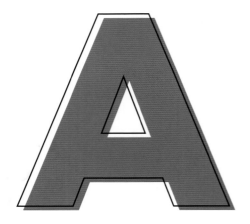

AQUAFABA

Aquafaba is a fancy name for the liquid in a can of beans that you most likely pour down the drain. Turns out, it's a fantastic plant-based, vegan egg replacer that was discovered back in 2015 by a guy named Goose Wohlt, who was asked to make vegan meringues for a Passover Seder. Meringues are traditionally made from whipped egg whites, so this presented quite a challenge. After some research and experimentation, tapping into earlier work done by a French gastronome named Joël Roessel, he found success.

Wohlt posted his win in a comment on Facebook—"dead simple delicious two ingredient whole food meringues . . . one can chickpea brine mixed w half cup sugar. perfect-O"—along with pictures of fluffy, white meringues. It went viral and, within days, everyone was in their kitchens whipping up meringue, including me.

Why did it work? A chemical analysis found that the liquid, or the brine, that results from cooking beans is similar in its chemical makeup to actual eggs, a combination of proteins, starches and saponins, which means it could do the same thing as eggs do in recipes, including emulsifying, coagulating and foaming. Wohlt started a revolution and needed a good name for it. He went with aquafaba, an amalgam of the Latin words for water and bean, because, let's face it, it sounds better.

Aquafaba from chickpeas, also known as garbanzo beans, is the best bean-water-as-egg-replacer. I have tried the brine from kidney beans, black beans and white beans. The brine from some white beans works, like cannellini, white kidney, great Northern and mayocoba, depending on the recipe, but not kidney and black beans. The brine is too dark and the flavor is way too strong. So, it's chickpeas all the way. In fact, the brine from chickpeas even looks like egg whites and, when it cooks up in a recipe, there is no trace of bean flavor.

Can you buy aquafaba at the market? Yes! It comes in a can of beans. Look for BPA-free cans with little or no sodium added. A 15-ounce (425-g) can contains about 1½ cups (246 g) of beans and ¾ cup (180 ml) of aquafaba. But if you are someone who likes to make your own beans from scratch, you are already making aquafaba. Just drain the beans, save the cooking liquid and reduce it down by half.

Now that you know all about aquafaba, it's time to start cooking with it. I have used it to make lox out of carrots and carpaccio out of beets, a clever way to use the starchy properties of aquafaba to transform the texture of the vegetables into cool new versions of themselves. And it's my favorite egg replacer for cookies and brownies. You can find those recipes in my first book, *Wait, That's Vegan?!*

I have also experimented with aquafaba in recipes that require an egg or two like pancakes, waffles and ice cream. But, to be honest, using aquafaba in those recipes is almost gratuitous because there are better ways to make all of those things, like my fluffy and amazing Banana-Quinoa Buttermilk Pancakes (page 121).

Where aquafaba really shines is in recipes that specifically rely on eggs or egg whites as the main ingredient, recipes that cannot be truly replicated with any other vegan egg replacer. That's why I am over the moon for Not Your Grandma's Gnocchi (page 11), Classic Coconut Macaroons (page 12) and Five-Minute Mayo (page 15).

And when you start experimenting on your own, whatever you make, just remember this: About 3 tablespoons (45 ml) of aquafaba equals one egg. Lightly shake or whisk aquafaba before using it. And always use aquafaba at room temperature.

NOT YOUR GRANDMA'S GNOCCHI

Over the years, I tried all different ways of making vegan gnocchi hoping for the same texture as the original, but I rarely had success worth bragging about. Until now. When I realized that aquafaba could successfully replace eggs to create soft, pillowy, perfect gnocchi, I was literally jumping for joy. I think this just might be the best recipe I have ever created!

Line a half sheet pan with parchment paper. Make room in the refrigerator for the sheet pan to sit flat.

Add the potatoes to a big pot and add enough cold water to cover them. Bring to a boil and cook until the potatoes are very tender, about 20 minutes. Drain the potatoes, put them back into the pot and shake them around to release the steam. Let them cool for a few minutes.

Pass the potatoes through a ricer or food mill over the sheet pan and spread them in an even layer. Place the sheet pan in the refrigerator to cool completely, at least 30 minutes.

Add the aquafaba to a small bowl and whisk just until it becomes foamy and white.

Take the potatoes out of the refrigerator. Lightly flour a clean work surface and turn out the potatoes onto the floured area. Sprinkle ½ cup (63 g) of the flour over the potatoes and bring them together to form a small mound. Make a little well in the center. Pour the aquafaba into the well and sprinkle 1 tablespoon (8 g) of flour over the top. Work everything together to form a crumbly dough. Sprinkle the remaining 1 tablespoon (8 g) of flour over the top and gently work to form a smooth, tight ball of dough.

Clean your work surface and line your sheet pan with a new piece of parchment paper. Use a bench scraper to divide the dough into 8 pieces. Use the palms of your hands to roll each ball into a rope, about ½ inch (1.3 cm) thick and 8 inches (20 cm) long. Use the bench scraper to cut each rope into ¾-inch (2-cm) pieces, cleaning the edge occasionally, and place the gnocchi on the sheet pan. Each rope should yield about 12 gnocchi.

Once all of the gnocchi are cut, decide on your plan of action. You can freeze the gnocchi or serve them immediately. If you are going to freeze them, place the sheet pan in the freezer as is. The gnocchi will freeze in about 30 minutes. Once frozen, transfer them to a freezer-safe container and store for up to 3 months. When ready to serve, follow the instructions below.

To cook the gnocchi, bring a big pot of salted water to a boil. When the water is boiling, drop the gnocchi (fresh or frozen) into the boiling water, adding only enough to cover the bottom of the pot, working in batches, as necessary. The gnocchi will float to the surface when they are done, about 1 to 2 minutes. Use a spider strainer or slotted spoon to lift them out of the water.

Serve immediately tossed in your favorite sauce.

Makes approximately 1 pound (454 g)

1 lb (454 g) russet potatoes (about 2 medium-sized potatoes), peeled and coarsely chopped

3 tbsp (45 ml) aquafaba, room temperature

½ cup (63 g) plus 2 tbsp (16 g) all-purpose flour, divided

Makes 20

MACAROONS

7 oz (198 g) unsweetened shredded coconut

7 oz (210 ml) sweetened condensed coconut milk

3 tbsp (45 ml) aquafaba, room temperature

1 tsp vanilla extract

¼ tsp salt

1 tbsp (8 g) vegan powdered sugar

CHOCOLATE

4 oz (113 g) plain vegan chocolate, finely chopped

ISN'T SUGAR VEGAN?

No, not all sugar is vegan because most commercial brands whiten sugar through a refining process that uses bone char—charred animal bones—which is considered a natural carbon, except it's from animals, which makes it undesirable for vegan cooking and baking. This includes powdered sugar, cane sugar and brown sugar (because brown sugar is white sugar with molasses added to it). So, look for brands that label their sugar "suitable for vegans."

CLASSIC COCONUT MACAROONS

These are like the kind of macaroons my family had growing up at our Passover Seders. They came in a can and I loved them! I took inspiration from an old Barefoot Contessa recipe and replaced egg whites with whipped aquafaba. The result? Crunchy on the outside, chewy on the inside macaroon perfection.

Melt some chocolate and dip the bottoms of the macaroons or drizzle the chocolate over the tops. Just be festive and fun and don't wait for Passover to make them. Actually, you can make them up to 3 months ahead of time and store them in the freezer!

This recipe is easy but specific. Use a kitchen scale to measure the shredded coconut, condensed milk and chocolate.

Preheat the oven to 350°F (177°C). Line a half sheet pan with parchment paper.

Add the shredded coconut and condensed coconut milk to a big mixing bowl. Mix well to coat all of the coconut with the coconut milk. Set aside.

Add the aquafaba, vanilla and salt to the bowl of a stand mixer fitted with a wire whip attachment or a big mixing bowl if using a hand mixer. Whip the mixture until it becomes opaque. Add the powdered sugar and continue whipping until it's glossy and soft peaks form, about 5 minutes.

Fold the whipped aquafaba into the coconut mixture and mix until thoroughly combined.

Use a 1-tablespoon (15-g) ice cream scooper to scoop out the mixture, pressing it on the side of the bowl to pack it well. Drop the scoops onto the sheet pan, leaving a bit of space in between each one.

Bake for 20 to 25 minutes, until golden brown all over. Remove from the oven and let them cool completely on the sheet pan.

To melt the chocolate, bring a small pot of water to a boil. Set a heatproof bowl over the boiling water and add two-thirds of the chocolate. Do not stir as the chocolate begins to melt.

Set a folded kitchen towel on the counter. When about three-quarters of the chocolate has melted, lift the bowl off the pot, turn off the heat and place the bowl on the kitchen towel. Add the remaining chocolate and gently stir until all of the chocolate is melted.

Dip the bottoms of the macaroons into the melted chocolate, letting any excess drip back into the bowl, and return the macaroons to the sheet pan. Alternatively, dip a fork into the chocolate and drizzle over the top of the macaroons. Or some combination of dipping and drizzling!

Place the macaroons in the refrigerator to set, at least 1 hour.

FIVE-MINUTE MAYO

Mayo is an emulsion made from oil, eggs, vinegar or lemon juice, and seasonings. I started making mayo with aquafaba as soon as I realized it was the ideal plant-based replacement for eggs. Not only is it quick and easy, but it's essentially free. Every time you open a can of beans or make beans from scratch, save the aquafaba so you can have mayo anytime you want it. Think of it as small-batch, artisanal mayo! Use an immersion blender for best mayo results.

Add the aquafaba to a 3-cup (720-ml) mixing vessel or a pint-sized (473-ml) wide-mouth jar. Insert an immersion blender and blend until the aquafaba is just frothy, about 5 seconds.

Add the maple syrup, vinegar, mustard powder, white pepper and salt and whip it for a second to incorporate.

Very slowly add the sunflower oil into the aquafaba mixture, blending as you go. The mixture will emulsify and thicken up. Once you have finished adding the oil, you will have mayo, about 5 minutes.

Store in an airtight container in the refrigerator and use within 1 week.

Makes approximately ¾ cup (180 ml)

---

3 tbsp (45 ml) aquafaba, room temperature

1 tsp maple syrup

1 tsp apple cider vinegar

¼ tsp mustard powder

¼ tsp white pepper

¼ tsp salt

¾ cup (180 ml) sunflower oil

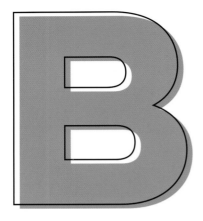

BEETS

Beets come in the prettiest colors—ruby red, purple, golden, white and, my favorite, pink-and-white candy cane stripes—and people either love them or hate them. The lovers say they taste earthy and sweet and sometimes a little bitter. The haters say they taste like dirt. That's pretty harsh, but there's a reason.

Beets contain a natural compound called geosmin that, for some people, makes them taste like wet earth, like the soil in a newly planted garden after a light rain. Are you one of those people? I totally get it. I think cilantro tastes like soap (more on that on page 56), but I have figured out a way to mitigate it. Same with beets. I have found ways to transform them in recipes that I am confident will turn beet haters into beet lovers.

Beets are said to be named after the Greek letter beta because they resemble a Greek "B." They were cultivated along the coast of the Mediterranean thousands of years ago, first for the leaves, then for the bulb. The ancient Romans used beets as an aphrodisiac and the Greeks believed that if two people shared a beet, they would fall in love. Awww.

Beets are incredibly healthy. They are high in fiber and loaded with almost all of the vitamins and minerals we need, including calcium, magnesium, potassium, iron and vitamins A, B and C. They are loaded with phytonutrients, which help reduce inflammation, and they are rich in nitrates, which are converted into nitric oxide during digestion. This process helps improve blood flow, lower blood pressure, reduce the risk of heart attacks and strokes and increase stamina and endurance. And beets are rich in boron, which plays a key role in the production of human sex hormones. Those Greeks and Romans. They knew it!

When you are out shopping for beets, look for ones that are firm to the touch, with their roots intact and that have bright green and crisp (not wilted) greens. You can buy them loose, but why not buy the whole plant? The greens are free! Cut them off when you get home, clean them really well (they tend to be very sandy) and treat them the same way you would any leafy green like kale, chard or spinach. Add them to a smoothie or sauté them with some good olive oil and garlic.

There are a lot of different ways to prepare beets. Just know that red beets bleed and stain everything—your hands, your cutting board, your white counter, your taco tortillas—but that shouldn't stop you from enjoying them in a myriad of ways. If you already love them, just shred one and add it to a salad like the Balsamic Tempeh Dragon Bowls (page 139), or thinly slice and pickle them, highlighting their inner beauty and transforming their texture, by using the pickling formula for Quick Pickles (page 152).

If you aren't there yet, ease into beet-lover status. Sauté shredded beets with jalapeños and Mexican oregano and turn them into really flavorful plant-based taco meat in Shredded Beet Tacos with Tomatillo Salsa (page 19), or roast them and make the herbaceous Lentil Salad with Roasted Beets and Fresh Herbs (page 86).

And if that doesn't do it for you, just hide some beets inside these fudgy, sweet Chocolate-Beet Cupcakes with Cream Cheese Frosting (page 20). No dirt, just decadence!

SHREDDED BEET TACOS WITH TOMATILLO SALSA

These tacos are inspired by machaca tacos, traditional Mexican shredded beef tacos. Sautéing shredded beets with onions, jalapeños, cumin and Mexican oregano transforms them into juicy, plant-based taco meat that is unique and full of flavor.

There are a lot of different ways to dress tacos, but there should always be some kind of salsa, a hit of acid and a little crunch. Here, they are topped with tomatillo salsa, Pickled Radishes (page 152) and toasted pumpkin seeds. But it's your taco party, so top them however you want!

Heat a pan with sides over medium-low heat. Add the sunflower oil. When it's shimmering, add the onions. Use tongs to mix the onions around and coat them with the oil. Cover the pan and sweat the onions until they soften and become translucent, about 8 minutes.

Uncover and add the garlic and jalapeño and cook until the garlic is fragrant, about 2 minutes.

Add the beets, Mexican oregano, cumin and chili powder. Mix to coat the beets with the spices. Add the water, cover and cook, stirring occasionally, until the beets are soft and have melded with the onion, about 10 minutes. If the mixture starts to stick to the pan, add a little bit more water.

In the meantime, prepare the tomatillo salsa. Add the tomatillos, onion and serrano pepper, cut side down, to a dry cast-iron or nonstick skillet. Set over medium heat and cook until the onion is charred and the tomatillos start to soften, 8 to 12 minutes. Take the pan off the heat and let cool.

Add the tomatillos, onion, serrano pepper, garlic, cilantro and salt to a blender. Pulse a few times until the mixture is chunky and then blend to your desired consistency.

Char the tortillas one at a time on an open flame or heat them on a dry cast-iron skillet.

To assemble the tacos, layer with beets and top with tomatillo salsa, lettuce, sour cream, Pickled Radishes and pumpkin seeds. Serve with lime wedges on the side.

SHREDDED BEET FILLING

1 tsp sunflower oil

½ red onion, thinly sliced into half-moons

1 clove garlic, pressed

1 jalapeño pepper, seeds and ribs removed and diced

1 big red beet, peeled and shredded

2 tsp (2 g) Mexican oregano

1 tsp cumin

½ tsp chili powder

¼ cup (60 ml) water

TOMATILLO SALSA

4 tomatillos, husks removed, rinsed and cut in half

½ white onion

1 serrano pepper, seeds and ribs removed and cut in half

1 clove garlic, peeled

¼ cup (4 g) lightly packed fresh cilantro leaves

Pinch of salt

TO SERVE

8 corn tortillas

Shredded romaine lettuce

Vegan sour cream

Pickled Radishes (page 152)

Toasted pumpkin seeds

Lime wedges

Makes 12

BEET PUREE

2 big or 4 small beets

CUPCAKES

1½ cups (188 g) all-purpose flour

¼ cup (22 g) cocoa powder

1 tsp baking soda

½ tsp salt

1 cup (192 g) vegan cane sugar

WET INGREDIENTS

1 cup (240 ml) cold water

1 tbsp (15 ml) apple cider vinegar

1 tsp vanilla extract

CREAM CHEESE FROSTING

½ cup (116 g) vegan cream cheese, room temperature

¼ cup (51 g) vegan shortening

2¼ cups (270 g) vegan powdered sugar, divided

Pinch of salt

CHOCOLATE-BEET CUPCAKES WITH CREAM CHEESE FROSTING

How do you get a beet hater to love beets? Make them these addicting fudgy chocolate cupcakes! Soft and buttery roasted beets are pureed and added to the mix, which does two things. One, they eliminate the need for oil or butter. Two, they bring out the best in the chocolate. The result? Sweet, moist cupcakes that don't taste like beets. At all.

Make this recipe even easier than it already is by roasting and pureeing the beets and making the frosting ahead of time. Both can be stored in an airtight container in the refrigerator for up to 1 week or in the freezer for up to 6 months.

To make the beet puree, preheat the oven to 400°F (204°C). Cut off the greens and trim the root end, but don't peel them. Place the beets on a piece of parchment paper on top of a piece of aluminum foil on a sheet pan and wrap them tightly. Roast small beets for 1 hour and big beets for 90 minutes, until they are tender enough for a knife to easily pass through them. Once the beets are cool enough to handle, peel the skin by pressing it lightly and rubbing it off. Let them cool completely.

To make the cupcakes, preheat the oven to 350°F (177°C). Place cupcake liners in each cupcake well.

Add the beets to the bowl of a small food processor and puree them until they are completely smooth. Measure out ½ cup (113 g) of the puree and set aside. If you have leftover puree, use it in a smoothie or freeze it for your next batch of cupcakes.

Add the flour, cocoa powder, baking soda and salt to a big mixing bowl. Whisk together, making sure there are no clumps. Add the beet puree, sugar, water, apple cider vinegar and vanilla. Mix, using a hand mixer on low, until the batter is smooth.

Add ¼ cup (57 g) of the batter to each cupcake liner. If there is any excess batter, distribute it evenly.

Bake for 25 to 30 minutes, or until a tester comes out clean. Let the cupcakes cool for a few minutes and then transfer them to a cooling rack to cool completely before frosting.

To make the frosting, place the cream cheese and shortening in a big mixing bowl. Use a hand mixer to whip them together until nice and creamy. Add about 1 cup (120 g) of powdered sugar and, with the mixer on low, mix to incorporate. Add the rest of the sugar and salt. Continue mixing until the frosting is smooth and fluffy, about 3 minutes.

Use an offset spatula or piping bag to frost the cupcakes.

COCONUT MILK

From Thailand to India and Hawaii to Jamaica, coconut milk is a staple ingredient in many cuisines around the world. It's very versatile and makes even the simplest recipes come to life. In the plant-based kitchen, coconut milk is both a dairy alternative and a flavor builder.

You may already know this, but coconut milk is not the liquid inside the coconut. That's coconut water, which has become super popular over the last decade. Coconut milk is its own thing, made by grating the flesh of the coconut, soaking it in hot water and pressing it through a cheesecloth, resulting in a shockingly bright white milk.

It is true that coconut milk is high in saturated fat and calories, but if you use it in moderation you will be fine. Plus, it is rich in antioxidants, iron, magnesium, potassium, copper and manganese.

When you are out shopping for coconut milk, be sure you are buying coconut milk for cooking, which generally comes in a can, and not coconut milk beverage, which is crafted to be more like a drinkable plant milk. Look for BPA-free cans that are labeled vegan. Many brands contain guar gum, a natural stabilizer made from milled guar beans. It thickens, emulsifies and stabilizes the coconut milk, making it extra smooth and creamy. Coconut milk without it tends to be oily and a little gross. Guar gum is totally fine, so don't worry about it.

There are different varieties of coconut milk, ranging in fat content. Full-fat coconut milk is high in fat and calories and thick, rich and creamy. Reduced-fat coconut milk has less fat and calories because it contains more water, which makes it lighter and less aggressively coconutty. Which one to use depends on the recipe you are making. They also make sweetened condensed coconut milk, which is made the same way as its dairy counterpart. It's super creamy, super sweet and super perfect in Classic Coconut Macaroons (page 12).

Coconut milk replaces dairy in Creamy Corn Chowder (page 25), creates a rich and satisfying cheese sauce for plant-based, dairy-free Classic Crusty Mac and Cheese (page 103) and Tofu Satay with Coconut-Peanut Sauce (page 26) cannot be made without it.

When it comes to dessert, coconut milk is magical. It makes dreamy Sweet Buttery Miso Caramel (page 95), creamy Chia-Hemp-Coconut Pudding Parfaits with Date Syrup (page 133) and those coconutty macaroons (page 12).

With so many ways to use coconut milk, you will need a steady supply, but if a recipe only calls for a portion of the can, don't stress! Store the leftover coconut milk in an airtight container in the refrigerator for up to 1 week or in the freezer for up to 6 months.

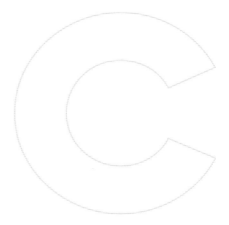

CREAMY CORN CHOWDER

A good corn chowder has to check a lot of boxes. It should be thick, rich, chunky, creamy, sweet and a little bit spicy all at the same time. Can it be done? Yes! Coconut milk stands in for dairy, adding a rich, thick, creamy sweetness. Aromatics like onions, leeks and garlic add depth of flavor and Aleppo pepper adds a light, bright fruity spiciness. And, of course, it's not corn chowder without lots of sweet corn and hearty potatoes. This is serious comfort food in a bowl and just as delicious as anything you have ever tasted.

Heat a heavy-bottomed soup pot over medium heat. Add the olive oil. When it's shimmering, add the onions, carrots and leeks, and cook until the vegetables start to soften, about 10 minutes. Add the garlic, Aleppo pepper, salt and pepper, and mix around and cook until the garlic is fragrant, about 1 minute.

Add the corn, potatoes, coconut milk and water and stir around. Add the thyme sprigs and bay leaf. Bring to a boil, reduce to a simmer and cook with the cover askew for 15 to 20 minutes, until the potatoes are tender.

Remove the thyme sprigs and bay leaf and stir in the butter and sherry vinegar.

Serve topped with chives and oyster crackers.

1 tbsp (15 ml) good olive oil

1 small onion, diced

1 carrot, cut into rounds

1 leek, white and light green parts, cleaned and cut into half-moons

2 cloves garlic, pressed

1 tsp Aleppo pepper

Pinch of salt

Dash of pepper

2 cups (308 g) fresh, canned or frozen sweet corn

2 Yukon gold potatoes, diced

1 (13.5-oz [400-ml]) can full-fat unsweetened coconut milk

1 cup (240 ml) water

3 sprigs fresh thyme

1 bay leaf

1 tbsp (14 g) vegan butter

1 tsp sherry vinegar

TO SERVE

Fresh chives, chopped

Oyster crackers

TOFU SATAY

1 tbsp (15 ml) tamari

1 tbsp (15 ml) sunflower oil

1 tbsp (15 ml) maple syrup

1 tbsp (15 ml) apple cider vinegar

1 tsp garlic powder

1 tsp ground ginger

Turmeric, a few shakes

1 (15-oz [425-g]) package extra-firm tofu, drained and pressed for 10 minutes and cut into 48 cubes

COCONUT-PEANUT SAUCE

½ cup (120 ml) reduced-fat unsweetened coconut milk

¼ cup (65 g) peanut butter, room temperature

1 tbsp (15 ml) tamari

1 tbsp (15 ml) fresh lime juice

2 tsp (8 g) coconut sugar

1 clove garlic, pressed

1 tsp grated fresh ginger

1 scallion, white and green parts, thinly sliced

TO SERVE

1 tsp toasted sesame seeds

Pickled Cucumbers (page 152)

TOFU SATAY WITH COCONUT-PEANUT SAUCE

Satay, a dish that originated in Java, Indonesia, was inspired by the kebabs of the Middle East. Traditionally, seasoned and skewered meat is served with a gravy or a sauce. In this version, tofu is seasoned, skewered and baked, highlighting just how meaty and flavorful tofu can be. But it's the dipping sauce that makes this dish. Creamy coconut milk is whisked together with dreamy peanut butter and fresh garlic and ginger. It's sweet and spicy and ridiculously delicious.

Preheat the oven to 400°F (204°C). Line a half sheet pan with parchment paper.

To prepare the tofu, add the tamari, sunflower oil, maple syrup, apple cider vinegar, garlic powder, ground ginger and turmeric to a big mixing bowl. Whisk to combine. Add the tofu cubes to the marinade and toss to coat. Thread 8 cubes onto each skewer and place on the sheet pan.

Bake for 40 to 45 minutes, until the tofu is golden brown and crispy around the edges.

In the meantime, make the coconut-peanut sauce. Add the coconut milk, peanut butter, tamari, lime juice, coconut sugar, garlic and ginger to a small pot. Cook over low heat, whisking constantly until the sauce is smooth and has thickened up, about 2 to 3 minutes. Turn off the heat and mix in the scallions. Turn out into a dipping bowl and let it cool.

Arrange the skewers on a platter. Sprinkle with sesame seeds and serve with coconut-peanut sauce and Pickled Cucumbers on the side.

WHAT IS TAMARI?

Tamari is Japanese soy sauce. It's similar to Chinese soy sauce, but different. Soy sauce is the liquid that is pressed out of a brewed and fermented mixture of soybeans and wheat. It's a one-note salty sauce. Tamari is the liquid that is extracted from fermented miso paste. It's thicker than soy sauce, less salty, more nuanced and rich in umami, which is why it's a great addition to your vegan pantry. It adds a rich, savory and mouthwatering flavor to all kinds of recipes. Plus, it's high in protein and antioxidants and naturally gluten-free. Look for it next to the soy sauce at the market.

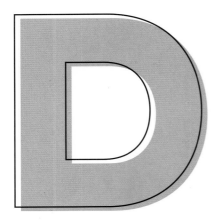

DATES

Dates are thought to be the oldest cultivated fruit in the world and one of the sweetest on the planet. There is evidence that date palm trees have existed for 50 million years and are thought to have originated in Mesopotamia, my favorite topic from 6th-grade social studies. Dates are mentioned in the Bible more than 50 times. In fact, the land of milk and honey? That honey is believed to be date syrup and not bee honey!

Dates are high in fructose—natural fruit sugar—which is low on the glycemic index, meaning sustained energy and not a blood sugar spike. They are rich in antioxidants, including flavonoids and carotenoids, which reduce inflammation and promote heart health, and they are high in protein and fiber, which keep you full and regular. They are also rich in magnesium, potassium and selenium, all good for bone health. Dates are also high in iron and rich in vitamins A, B and C.

So, don't let people tell you that they are unhealthy and full of sugar. Tell them that they are super healthy and full of natural fruit sugar!

It's hard to describe exactly what dates taste like. They are dense, moist, sticky and sweet, like a cross between raisins and prunes and figs but with a kind of rich and buttery caramel flavor. Go ahead and try one straight up. Right?! Now, if you really want a fun snack, stuff them with a little peanut butter, almond butter, tahini, vegan cream cheese or whatever else you can think of. I always add two to my daily smoothie, for both sweetness and fiber.

When dates are cooked down, a little or a lot, the flavors become concentrated, the texture changes and they add something really special to whatever sweet or savory recipe you are making.

In Old-Fashioned Date and Nut Bread (page 31), they are soft and chewy little bites of sweetness. In Delicious Date-Oat Squares (page 46), they are transformed into a jammy filling. In Caponata with Dates and Two Vinegars (page 32), a unique take on the classic sweet and sour vegetable jam, they add sweetness. And when dates are cooked down all the way, strained and reduced, they are completely transformed into that biblical honey, Date Syrup (page 133).

OLD-FASHIONED DATE AND NUT BREAD

Move over, banana bread, there is a new quick bread in town. Actually, it's not that new. Date and nut bread originated in Scotland over a hundred years ago and became a popular staple in many homes. My grandmother always had a plate of fresh-out-of-the-oven date and nut bread waiting for us whenever we arrived for a visit. She taught me how to make it and, when I went vegan, I reinvented her recipe using flax eggs and coconut sugar. It's just as sweet, moist, dark and memorable as the original. It's especially enjoyable with a schmear of vegan cream cheese.

Preheat the oven to 350°F (177°C). Lightly brush two mini loaf pans or one big loaf pan with oil.

To make the flax egg, whisk together the ground flaxseed and water in a small mixing bowl. Set aside for 5 minutes to thicken.

To prepare the fruit, add the water, dates and raisins to a small pot. Bring to a boil and immediately turn off the heat. Add the baking soda and quickly whisk it into the fruit. Be careful; it will bubble up. Set aside for 5 minutes.

Add the flax egg, sunflower oil and vanilla to the fruit and mix well.

Add the flour, coconut sugar, walnuts and salt to a big mixing bowl. Add the fruit mixture and mix until a batter forms and all of the flour is incorporated. It will be sticky.

If you are making two mini loaves, spoon half of the batter into each mini loaf pan. Bake for 35 to 40 minutes, or until the tops have puffed up and a tester comes out clean.

If you are making one standard loaf, spoon all of the batter into the loaf pan. Bake for 65 to 80 minutes, or until the top has puffed up and a tester comes out clean.

Let the loaves or loaf cool for a few minutes and then transfer them to a cooling rack to cool completely before slicing.

If not serving immediately, wrap them in plastic wrap and store in the refrigerator for up to 1 week or in the freezer for up to 6 months.

Makes 2 mini loaves or 1 standard loaf

FLAX EGG

1 tbsp (10 g) ground flaxseed

3 tbsp (45 ml) water

FRUIT

1 cup (240 ml) water

½ cup (40 g) pitted and finely chopped Medjool dates

½ cup (73 g) Thompson or golden raisins (or a combination of both)

1 heaping tsp baking soda

2 tbsp (30 ml) sunflower oil, plus more for brushing

1 tsp vanilla extract

1½ cups (188 g) all-purpose flour

½ cup (96 g) coconut sugar

½ cup (59 g) chopped walnuts

½ tsp salt

Serves 4 to 6

4 tbsp (60 ml) good olive oil, divided

1 small red onion, thinly sliced into quarter moons

1 small eggplant, diced

1 small zucchini, diced

2 ribs celery, diced

2 cloves garlic, pressed

Pinch of salt

1 tbsp (16 g) tomato paste

1 cup (240 g) jarred diced tomatoes

½ cup (40 g) pitted and finely chopped Medjool dates

½ cup (90 g) pitted green olives, cut in half

2 tbsp (18 g) capers, drained

2 tbsp (30 ml) red wine vinegar

1 tbsp (12 g) coconut sugar

1 tbsp (15 ml) good balsamic vinegar

TO SERVE

Fresh parsley, chopped

Fresh mint, chopped

Crusty bread

CAPONATA WITH DATES AND TWO VINEGARS

Caponata is a traditional Sicilian dish, a kind of sweet and sour vegetable jam. I thought it would be interesting to add dates as the sweet element. And they totally work! They are cooked down with eggplant and zucchini, savory olives and capers, and then seasoned with two different vinegars, each bringing their own unique flavor—the sour part of the equation—to the table.

Heat a big pan with sides over medium heat. Add 2 tablespoons (30 ml) of olive oil. When it's shimmering, add the onions, eggplant, zucchini, celery, garlic and salt. Cook, stirring occasionally, until the vegetables are very tender, about 15 minutes. Add the remaining 2 tablespoons (30 ml) of oil and stir it into the vegetables.

Add the tomato paste. Use a wooden spoon to mix the tomato paste into the onion mixture, cooking it for 3 to 4 minutes.

Add the diced tomatoes, dates, olives and capers. Season with red wine vinegar and coconut sugar. Reduce the heat to low, cover and stew for 20 to 25 minutes, stirring occasionally until the caponata has thickened and everything has melded together.

Take the pan off the heat and stir in the balsamic vinegar.

Serve warm or at room temperature, topped with parsley and mint and served with crusty bread on the side.

WHAT IS COCONUT SUGAR?

Coconut sugar is made from the sap of the coconut palm tree, the same tree that produces the coconuts that produce coconut milk. The sap is heated until the water evaporates, resulting in a caramel-color granulated natural sweetener that tastes like a cross between caramel, maple syrup and brown sugar. Coconut sugar is unrefined, low on the glycemic index—meaning sustained energy, not a blood sugar spike—and it contains trace amounts of health-promoting phytonutrients and antioxidants. And, it's automatically vegan!

EGGPLANT

Eggplant is a delicious and nutrient-dense ingredient. It comes in a variety of shapes, sizes and colors, from the ubiquitous dark purple globe eggplant to the skinny Chinese and Japanese varieties to the little multicolor fairy-tale ones. Did you know they also come in white? That's the eggplant that inspired the name because it looks like a big goose egg!

Eggplant is low in calories and high in fiber, which is crucial for both heart and gastrointestinal health. Eggplant is also a great source of vitamins, minerals and antioxidants, including vitamins C, K and B6, thiamine, niacin, magnesium, manganese, phosphorus, copper, fiber, folic acid and potassium.

When you are out shopping for eggplant, look for ones that have smooth, shiny skin and a bright green stem attached to a pretty star-shaped flower. They should feel heavy and firm to the touch. When you cut them open, the flesh will vary from a light creamy color to a light greenish hue with little brown spots around the seeds. If the flesh is more brown than white though, the eggplant is past its prime and exceedingly bitter. Trust me, I know this from experience.

The dense, spongy flesh of eggplant has quite a unique texture that has to be cooked in order to be eaten and, depending on the recipe, might have to be salted. While there is some debate as to whether or not it's necessary, I think there is good reason to and here's why.

The original reason for salting or sweating an eggplant before cooking was because, at one time, eggplant was excessively bitter tasting and salting drew out the bitterness; however, that isn't really necessary anymore because the bitterness has been cultivated out of eggplant. But, salting does something else. It draws out water, collapsing the air pockets in the spongy flesh and preventing the eggplant from absorbing too much oil. The result? Soft and creamy—not oily—eggplant!

For recipes that call for grilling, roasting or pan-frying, salting is a must. Not only does the eggplant taste better, but it tends to cook more quickly. Prep the eggplant according to the recipe, cutting it into whatever shape you desire—rounds, steaks, cubes—and generously sprinkle the flesh with salt.

Lay the eggplant in a single layer on paper towel–lined sheet pans and top with another layer of paper towels, making as many layers as needed. Let the eggplant sit for at least one hour and then pat it dry before proceeding with your recipe.

Salting takes a little extra time, but it's worth it in the end. You will see why in recipes like Miso Eggplant (page 37) and Eggplant Steaks with Chimichurri (page 38). If the recipe doesn't call for salting, it isn't necessary because the water is useful to the cooking process, like when cooking eggplant on the stove-top. You will see it in action when you make Caponata with Dates and Two Vinegars (page 32) and Spaghetti with Eggplant Bolognese (page 41).

MISO EGGPLANT

Miso eggplant, nasu dengaku, is a popular Japanese dish. It's an appetizer on the menu at Japanese restaurants everywhere, but it's just as easy to make at home. First, the eggplant is roasted, so the flesh softens up, then it's broiled so the miso caramelizes into a sticky, sweet and salty glaze. It's so good, you might just skip dinner.

EGGPLANT

4 Japanese or Chinese eggplants

Salt

Sunflower oil, for brushing

MISO GLAZE

2 tbsp (30 ml) mellow white miso

1 tbsp (15 ml) sunflower oil

1 tbsp (15 ml) mirin

1 tbsp (15 ml) tamari

1 tbsp (15 ml) apple cider vinegar

TO SERVE

2 scallions, white and green parts, thinly sliced

2 tsp (4 g) toasted sesame seeds

Line a sheet pan with paper towels. Cut the eggplants in half lengthwise. To score the flesh, use a paring knife to cut diagonal lines about 1 inch (2.5 cm) apart, without cutting through the skin. Turn and cut diagonal lines in the other direction, resulting in a diamond pattern. Generously salt the eggplants and lay them flesh side down. Let the eggplants sit for at least 1 hour.

Preheat the oven to 400°F (204°C). Line a half sheet pan with parchment paper.

Pat the eggplants with a clean paper towel to absorb any remaining water. Lightly brush the eggplants all over with sunflower oil and place them cut side down on the sheet pan. Bake for 20 minutes, until the flesh is soft and golden brown.

In the meantime, make the miso glaze. In a small mixing bowl, add the miso, sunflower oil, mirin, tamari and apple cider vinegar. Break up the miso with a small silicone spatula and whisk it together until completely smooth.

Take the eggplants out of the oven and turn the oven to the broiler setting.

Turn the eggplants over and brush the flesh with the miso glaze, coating the entire surface. Broil until the glaze has caramelized and is charred in spots, about 5 to 8 minutes.

Serve topped with scallions and sesame seeds.

Serves 4 to 6

EGGPLANT STEAKS

2 globe eggplants

Salt

Olive oil, for brushing

Dash of pepper

CHIMICHURRI

2 cloves garlic, pressed

1 small shallot, finely diced

1 red cherry pepper, deseeded and finely diced

2 tbsp (30 ml) red wine vinegar

2 tbsp (30 ml) fresh lemon juice

1 cup (60 g) finely chopped fresh parsley

½ cup (120 ml) good olive oil

½ tsp dried oregano

Pinch of salt

Dash of pepper

TO SERVE

Lemon wedges

EGGPLANT STEAKS WITH CHIMICHURRI

Chimichurri is a specialty sauce from Argentina that is bursting with flavor. Depending on who you believe, chimichurri either means "a mix of things in no special order" or "Jimmy's curry." I have to say, I like both! Either way, chimichurri is a bright green herbaceous sauce made with lots of parsley and vinegar and, in this version, a red cherry pepper, for some heat.

While it's traditionally served over grilled steak, here in plant city, it's served over grilled eggplant steaks. The combination of fresh herbs and the smoky char from the grill is so, so good. And on top of that, it's pretty!

Line a sheet pan with paper towels. Trim the top of the eggplants to remove the stems and leaves. Cut them into ¼-inch (6-mm)-thick steaks. Generously salt the steaks and lay them flesh side down. Let them sit for at least 1 hour. While they are sitting, prepare the chimichurri.

Add the garlic, shallots and red cherry peppers to a medium mixing bowl. Cover with the red wine vinegar and lemon juice and let sit for 15 minutes to macerate.

Add the parsley, olive oil, oregano, salt and pepper to the garlic-shallot-pepper mixture. Mix well. Marinate for at least 15 minutes.

To cook the eggplant steaks, heat a grill pan over medium heat or heat an actual grill. Pat the steaks with a clean paper towel to absorb any remaining water. Lightly brush one side with oil and season with pepper. Place them oil side down on the grill.

Grill until the steaks start to soften, lift up easily and you see grill marks, anywhere from 3 to 7 minutes, depending on how you are cooking them. Turn them halfway through to get crosshatch marks, if desired. Flip and grill the other side for another 3 minutes.

Arrange the eggplant steaks on a platter and drizzle with the chimichurri. Serve with lemon wedges on the side.

SPAGHETTI WITH EGGPLANT BOLOGNESE

Serves 4

What's better than a bowl of spaghetti smothered in a hearty Bolognese sauce? Not much! A traditional Bolognese is made with meat, but in this version, eggplant is the star of the show. Its rich and velvety texture is the perfect stand-in for ground meat. Made with all of the elements of the classic—and in a fraction of the time—the end result is a rich and delicious restaurant-level sauce that is perfect for a family-style pasta dinner. And to make life even easier, make this sauce ahead of time and store in an airtight container in the refrigerator for up to 1 week or in the freezer for up to 6 months.

Heat a big pan with sides over medium heat. Add 1 tablespoon (15 ml) of olive oil. When it's shimmering, add the eggplant, onions, carrots, celery, garlic, oregano, crushed red pepper and salt. Cook, stirring occasionally, until the vegetables are tender, about 10 minutes. Add the remaining oil and stir it into the vegetables.

Deglaze the pan with the white wine and cook until the wine is mostly absorbed, about 2 minutes.

Add the tomato paste. Use a wooden spoon to mix the tomato paste into the vegetables, cooking it for 3 to 4 minutes.

Add the tomatoes and gently break them up with the wooden spoon, leaving it as chunky as you like. Reduce the heat to low, cover and cook for 10 minutes, stirring occasionally and breaking up the tomatoes more, if you like. Take it off the heat and stir in the sherry vinegar.

In the meantime, bring a big pot of salted water to a boil and cook the spaghetti according to the package instructions. Drain and add the spaghetti to the Bolognese and mix well.

Serve topped with basil and Seedy Sprinkle Cheese.

2 tbsp (30 ml) good olive oil, divided

1 medium-sized eggplant, cut into ¼-inch (6-mm) dice

1 small onion, finely diced

1 big carrot, finely diced

1 rib celery, finely diced

2 cloves garlic, pressed

1 tsp oregano

¼ tsp crushed red pepper

Pinch of salt

½ cup (120 ml) vegan white wine

¼ cup (66 g) tomato paste

1 (18.3-oz [519-g]) jar whole peeled tomatoes

1 tsp sherry vinegar

½ lb (226 g) uncooked spaghetti

TO SERVE

Fresh basil, cut in chiffonade

Seedy Sprinkle Cheese (page 79)

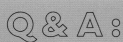

Q & A :

ISN'T WINE AUTOMATICALLY VEGAN BECAUSE IT IS MADE FROM GRAPES?

Nope. During the fining stage of winemaking, when the wine is clarified and stabilized, it may be processed using animal products such as casein (milk protein), albumin (egg whites), chitin (crustacean shells), gelatin (boiled animal parts) and isinglass (fish bladders). Vegan or not, that all sounds kind of gross. Luckily, there are a lot of winemakers nowadays using fining agents that are vegan-friendly, things such as bentonite clay, activated charcoal and limestone. That all sounds edgy and cool. So when you are out shopping for wine, ask the salespeople at the liquor store or search for vegan wine online.

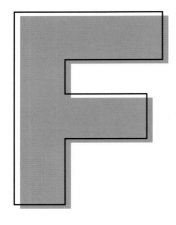

FLAXSEED

Flax is one of the oldest crops in the world. It was originally domesticated in the Fertile Crescent and has been cultivated for many different uses over the millennia. It has been used to make clothing, burial shrouds, rugs, ropes, tablecloths, bed linens and paper currency. Today, flax is grown all over the world and, for a few weeks each year, flax fields bloom with gorgeous bluish-purple flowers that look like a reflection of the sky.

The flaxseed we eat are harvested from inside little pods that grow along the stalks of the plant. They are either brown or golden and are little nutritional powerhouses. They are rich in omega-3s and have been shown to improve heart health and lower the risk of stroke. They are high in lignans, a powerful antioxidant, which has been shown to lower the risk of breast and prostate cancer. And, they are high in protein and dietary fiber.

Most nutrition experts recommend eating ground flaxseed versus whole flaxseed, because whole flaxseed pass through the intestines undigested, which defeats the whole purpose of eating them in the first place. An easy way to get them into your diet is to add ground flaxseed to a smoothie or a salad. The flavor is very mild, maybe slightly nutty, but not really that noticeable.

An even more fun way to get flaxseed into your diet is to use them as an egg replacer. In fact, it's the OG vegan egg substitute! Unlike aquafaba, flax eggs are not chemically similar to actual eggs, but when they are whisked with water and left to sit for a bit, they become gelatinous. Then, when added to certain recipes, they do the work that eggs do. While they are never going to perform exactly like eggs, they don't need to. Trust me, when you take a bite out of any of these recipes, you will never, not once, miss the eggs.

Flax eggs work really well in baked goods because they provide just enough structure and a little density, like in quick breads, cakes and crusts. You will see the vegan magic in action when you make Banana-Caramel Upside-Down Cake (page 45), Delicious Date-Oat Squares (page 46) and Old-Fashioned Date and Nut Bread (page 31).

In other types of recipes, flax eggs provide moisture and act as a binder, like in Zucchini-Dill Pancakes with Lemon-Chive Aioli (page 185) and Umeboshi Vinaigrette (page 181). And speaking of zucchini, if you have a recipe for zucchini bread, try making it with flax eggs next time!

Get to know flax eggs well. To make one, whisk together 1 tablespoon (10 g) of ground flaxseed with 3 tablespoons (45 ml) of water, and let it sit for at least 5 minutes so the flax can absorb the water and gelatinize. Flax eggs can turn some of your old favorites into new vegan versions of themselves.

BANANA-CARAMEL UPSIDE-DOWN CAKE

This is one of the most striking desserts you will ever see. Just look at that swirl of caramelly bananas! Underneath all of that gooey sweet goodness, you will find a deliciously light and slightly tangy white cake made with flax eggs and yogurt. Oh. My. Goodness. It's kind of perfect.

One more thing: The bananas might turn pink. They are totally fine to eat and kind of festive, so don't worry!

Preheat the oven to 350°F (177°C). Line a 9-inch (23-cm) springform pan or baking pan with a parchment round.

To make the flax eggs, whisk together the ground flaxseed and water in a small mixing bowl. Set aside for 5 minutes to thicken.

Pour the Sweet Buttery Miso Caramel into the pan and use an offset spatula or the back of a spoon to spread it in a thin layer as close to the edges as you can. Lay the bananas on top of the caramel, with their flat sides facing down and their rounded sides facing up, so when the cake is flipped upside down, the cut side will be facing up. Set aside.

Add the flour, baking soda, zest and salt to a big mixing bowl. Add the flax eggs, yogurt, sugar, sunflower oil, lemon juice and vanilla. Mix, using a hand mixer on low, until the batter is smooth.

Pour the batter over the bananas. Bake for 60 to 75 minutes, or until the top is golden brown and a tester comes out clean.

Let the cake sit for at least 30 minutes. Carefully invert the cake onto a serving platter and release the springform pan or tap the top to release the cake. Remove the parchment round. Cool completely before serving.

FLAX EGGS

2 tbsp (20 g) ground flaxseed

6 tbsp (90 ml) water

BANANAS AND CARAMEL

¼ cup (60 ml) Sweet Buttery Miso Caramel (page 95)

3 big or 4 small ripe bananas, sliced lengthwise

CAKE

1½ cups (188 g) all-purpose flour

1 tsp baking soda

1 tsp lemon zest

½ tsp salt

1 cup (240 ml) plain unsweetened vegan yogurt

1 cup (192 g) vegan cane sugar

½ cup (120 ml) sunflower oil

1 tbsp (15 ml) fresh lemon juice

2 tsp (10 ml) vanilla extract

DELICIOUS DATE-OAT SQUARES

These soft and chewy squares are like a cross between a shortbread and a fruit crumble. Dates are cooked down and flavored up with vanilla and musky balsamic vinegar, transforming them into a jammy spread that is sandwiched between layers of buttery crust made with flax eggs and coconut oil. One bite and you are going to fall in love with the unique flavor and yummy texture. Wrap up these squares and keep them in an airtight container in the refrigerator (or freezer) to serve for dessert, but honestly, you could also eat them for breakfast or a snack anytime.

DATE FILLING

1 cup (80 g) pitted and chopped Medjool dates

½ cup (120 ml) water

1 tbsp (12 g) coconut sugar

1 tsp good balsamic vinegar

1 tsp vanilla extract

FLAX EGGS

2 tbsp (20 g) ground flaxseed

6 tbsp (90 ml) water

CRUST

1 cup (125 g) all-purpose flour

1 cup (90 g) old-fashioned rolled oats

½ cup (96 g) coconut sugar

½ tsp salt

½ cup (120 ml) melted refined coconut oil

To prepare the date filling, add the dates and water to a small pot. Bring to a boil, reduce to a high simmer and cook until the dates have broken down and transformed into a thick jam, about 10 minutes. Use a wooden spoon to break up the dates, as necessary. Take it off the heat and stir in the coconut sugar, balsamic vinegar and vanilla.

Preheat the oven to 350°F (177°C). Line an 8 x 8–inch (20.5 x 20.5–cm) brownie pan with parchment paper.

To make the flax eggs, whisk together the ground flaxseed and water in a small mixing bowl. Set aside for 5 minutes to thicken.

To make the crust, add the flour, oats, coconut sugar and salt to a big mixing bowl. Mix together. Add the flax eggs and coconut oil and mix to combine.

Spoon about two-thirds of the crust mixture into the pan. Spread it out into an even layer, pressing it to the edges. Spread the date filling over the top in a thin layer. Crumble the remaining crust mixture over the date filling.

Bake for 30 minutes.

Let it cool for a few minutes. Lift by the parchment paper and transfer it to a cooling rack to cool completely before cutting it into squares.

GARBANZO BEANS

Garbanzo beans are probably the number one bean consumed around the world. They were cultivated in the Middle East 10,000 years ago and were one of the first legumes to be eaten by humans. They are a common ingredient in everyday cooking in many cultures and are known by different names depending on where you are and what you are eating—such as chickpeas in the United States, chana in India and ceci in Italy.

Garbanzo beans are nutrient-dense, high in antioxidants, rich in dietary fiber and one amino acid short of being a complete protein. They are a great source of B vitamins, magnesium, iron and potassium, which boost heart health; they are high in saponins, which may help prevent the development of certain cancers; and they contain lots of iron and calcium, which contribute to healthy bones.

Not only that, but garbanzo beans are good for your financial health! Cans of garbanzo beans are cheap—and bags of dried beans are even cheaper.

Garbanzo beans are an all-around, easy-to-work-with ingredient that can be eaten hot or cold. They are probably most famous as hummus (page 52), so if you are not already making your own, you need to start right now.

Add garbanzo beans to salads like The Big Kale Salad with Seedy Sprinkle Cheese (page 79). Serve them with rice, quinoa or other whole grains. Sauté them with garlic and kale. Add them to soups like Green Minestrone (page 182) and pasta dishes like As-Spicy-as-You-Want-It Pasta e Ceci (page 55).

Have you seen bags of roasted garbanzo beans at the market? They are a fun and crunchy snack and you can make your own and season them any way you want. In the Deconstructed Falafel Salad with Hummus and Tahini Dressing (page 52), they are roasted to crispy perfection with falafel spices, but try nutritional yeast for a cheesy flavor, cayenne pepper for some spice or cinnamon and coconut sugar for a sweet treat.

One more thing: They also make garbanzo bean flour. Also known as besan, gram flour and chickpea flour, it's somewhat neutral, sort of nutty, low in calories, high in protein, packed with fiber, naturally gluten-free and used in recipes like socca, farinata, papadum and pakora. I use it to make Mushroom Omelets (page 66) and Zucchini-Dill Pancakes with Lemon-Chive Aioli (page 185). But whatever you do, don't taste it raw. It's bitter and awful. Don't worry, though, by the time it's thoroughly cooked, it's delicious!

FALAFEL-SPICED GARBANZO BEANS

1½ cups (246 g) cooked or 1 (15-oz [425-g]) can garbanzo beans, skins removed and patted completely dry

1 tbsp (15 ml) good olive oil

½ tsp cumin

½ tsp coriander

½ tsp sumac

½ tsp Aleppo pepper

¼ tsp garlic powder

¼ tsp onion powder

¼ tsp paprika

Pinch of salt

HUMMUS

1½ cups (246 g) cooked or 1 (15-oz [425-g]) can garbanzo beans, aquafaba reserved

1 clove garlic

2 tbsp (30 ml) fresh lemon juice

1 tbsp (15 ml) tahini

1 tbsp (15 ml) good olive oil

Pinch of salt

TAHINI DRESSING

¼ cup (60 ml) good tahini

2 tbsp (30 ml) fresh lemon juice

1 clove garlic, pressed

3 to 4 tbsp (45 to 60 ml) water

1 tsp chopped fresh parsley

Pinch of salt

SALAD

1 head romaine lettuce, chopped

2 Persian cucumbers, thinly sliced

12 mixed cherry or grape tomatoes, halved

¼ cup (40 g) diced red onion

2 tbsp (2 g) chopped fresh cilantro

2 tbsp (8 g) chopped fresh parsley

2 tbsp (7 g) chopped fresh dill

TO SERVE

Sumac or paprika

Yogurt Flatbread (page 175)

DECONSTRUCTED FALAFEL SALAD WITH HUMMUS AND TAHINI DRESSING

No need to go to all of the trouble to make actual falafels, those deep-fried Middle Eastern chickpea balls, with all of that oil and frying. Instead, take the easy way out and season garbanzo beans with all of the falafel spices and roast them up in the oven. They are a fun, crunchy snack all on their own but are even better on top of a big salad. Make them a day or two ahead of time so this salad is on the table in no time.

And while the garbanzos are baking, make your own hummus. There is absolutely no reason to buy hummus at the market when you can make it fresh at home in your food processor! And get creative. Season it with cumin, cayenne or za'atar. Add roasted vegetables like beets, carrots and red peppers. Or, really go crazy and replace the garbanzo beans with white or black beans!

Preheat the oven to 350°F (177°C). Line a half sheet pan with parchment paper.

To make the falafel-spiced garbanzo beans, add the garbanzo beans to a medium mixing bowl. Drizzle with the olive oil and toss to coat. Add the cumin, coriander, sumac, Aleppo pepper, garlic powder, onion powder, paprika and salt. Toss well to coat with the spices.

Turn out onto the sheet pan and bake for 1 hour, until the garbanzos start to look dry. Turn off the oven and leave them for at least 2 hours to be sure they are all completely dry and crispy.

To make the hummus, add the garbanzo beans, garlic, lemon juice, tahini, olive oil and salt to the bowl of a small food processor. Pulse a few times, scraping down the sides of the bowl, as necessary. To achieve your desired level of creaminess, add aquafaba 1 tablespoon (15 ml) at a time, and keep processing until you are happy with the texture.

To make the tahini dressing, add the tahini, lemon juice and garlic to a small mixing bowl. Mix together. The tahini will seize up. Add the water 1 tablespoon (15 ml) at a time, and continue mixing until the tahini loosens up and you have achieved your desired level of thickness. Add the parsley and season with salt.

To assemble the salad, arrange the lettuce on a big salad platter or in individual salad bowls. Top with the garbanzo beans, cucumbers, tomatoes and onions. Sprinkle with cilantro, parsley and dill and drizzle with the tahini dressing.

Add the hummus to a small bowl and sprinkle with sumac or paprika. Serve flatbreads on the side.

AS·SPICY·AS·YOU·WANT·IT PASTA E CECI

Pasta e ceci is a traditional Roman pasta and garbanzo bean stew. It's the kind of homey dish that has as many variations as households. So, that means there are a million ways to make it and this is mine. It starts with sautéed onions and garlic, because everything good starts with onions and garlic, and ends with a light tomato sauce made with nutritional yeast and umeboshi paste. Add as much crushed red pepper as you like to make it as spicy as you want it. The end result? A kind of grown-up, healthy version of SpaghettiOs®!

1 tbsp (15 ml) good olive oil

1 small onion, diced

2 cloves garlic, pressed

½ to 1 tsp crushed red pepper

Pinch of salt

Dash of pepper

¼ cup (66 g) tomato paste

1 tbsp (5 g) nutritional yeast

1 tbsp (18 g) umeboshi paste

1½ cups (246 g) cooked or 1 (15-oz [425-g]) can garbanzo beans, drained

2 cups (480 ml) water

¼ lb (113 g) uncooked anelletti or other small pasta

TO SERVE

Fresh basil, cut in chiffonade

Heat a heavy-bottomed soup pot over medium heat. Add the olive oil. When it's shimmering, add the onions and cook until they become translucent, about 5 minutes. Add the garlic, crushed red pepper, salt and pepper; mix around and cook until the garlic is fragrant, about 1 minute.

Add the tomato paste, nutritional yeast and umeboshi paste. Use a wooden spoon to mix it around, cooking the tomato paste for 3 to 4 minutes.

Add the beans and water and stir around. Cook with the cover askew for 15 minutes.

In the meantime, bring a big pot of salted water to a boil and cook the anelletti according to the package instructions. Drain and add the anelletti to the beans and mix well.

Serve topped with basil.

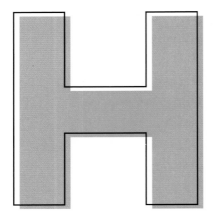

HERBS

For a long time, I thought herbs were extra, a throwaway ingredient, scattered about for decoration on meals ordered at a restaurant. But herbs are not just the domain of gourmet chefs and fancy recipes; they are the key to flavor town. Just a small handful of herbs can transform a dish in a way that almost no other ingredient can. From peppery parsley to cooling mint to oniony chives, different herbs bring their own unique flavors to the table. If you are not already cooking with them, now is the time to start.

There are two categories of herbs: soft and hard. Your job is to get to know what each herb tastes like, how they flavor a dish and when to add them to your cooking.

Soft herbs are bright green with tender leaves. There are many, but the ones that you will find throughout this book include parsley, cilantro, mint, basil, chives and dill.

Parsley is clean, fresh, mild and sort of grassy, in the best way possible. Sprinkling fresh parsley over the top of almost any dish adds a subtle freshness that rounds out and deepens all the rest of the flavors.

Cilantro is bright and citrusy, and quite distinctive. Some people say it tastes like soap. I am one of those people. We are genetically predisposed to detect aldehydes—a compound found in cilantro that is also produced during the making of soap. I find that if I pair cilantro with mint and other herbs, it's not nearly as intense. If you don't have this issue, you can increase the amount of cilantro in a recipe and leave out the other herbs altogether. It's totally up to you!

Mint is cool and sort of sweet and adds a bright, fresh note to any dish. Basil is peppery with a mild anise flavor and is one of the best herbs to pair with tomatoes. Chives have a delicate onion flavor, with a hint of garlic. They make a wonderfully light and pretty garnish.

Dill is kind of sweet, slightly bitter and sort of lemony with hints of grass and celery. It's really pretty, with feathery soft fronds that sometimes border on a bluish tone. It's a match made in culinary heaven with beets, lentils and mushrooms, to name a few.

Soft herbs should always be fresh, unless they are part of a dried herb mix. It should go without saying, but I will say it anyway: Always, always use fresh herbs for garnishes and when showcasing them in herb-centric recipes such as Savory Herb Butter (page 59), Rosemary-Chocolate Bark (page 60) and Chimichurri (page 38).

Hard herbs are woody, with firm dark green leaves and hearty stems. They tend to be more intense in flavor than soft herbs. There are many, but the ones you will find in this book include rosemary, thyme, oregano, Mexican oregano and bay leaves.

Hard herbs can be fresh or dried, but dried are more concentrated in flavor than fresh ones. So if you need to sub dried for fresh in a recipe, use 1 teaspoon of dried herbs for every 1 tablespoon (3 g) of fresh herbs. And if you are using dried herbs, rub them between your fingers or palms as you add them to the pot, so their natural oils are released.

Rosemary is bold and intense. It's piney, lemony, sharp and can easily overpower a dish. Thyme is gentle and lovely. It's herbal, a little minty and a little lemony.

Oregano is pungent with hints of mint. Mexican oregano is stronger than plain oregano, woodsier with a hint of citrusy lime. Of all of the hard herbs, oregano is the only one I would say dried is preferable to fresh.

Bay leaves are the difference between a good dish and a great one. On their own, bay leaves have an almost eucalyptus flavor, but when they cook down in soups, stews and sauces, they add a subtle layer of flavor that you can't necessarily identify, but, if it wasn't there, you would know something was missing. Fresh bay leaves are more intense than dried ones, but they are pretty much interchangeable.

One more thing: The vibrant green color of fresh herbs should tip you off that they are healthy. Every single one is rich in nutrients and packed with vitamins, minerals and antioxidants. But their true power lies in their abundance of polyphenols—plant compounds that help scavenge and neutralize free radicals and restore balance to the body, improving overall health and helping to combat diseases like cancer, heart disease, Alzheimer's and diabetes. So add them for flavor, add them for prettiness and add them for your health. It's a win-win-win!

Q & A :
WHAT IS THE BEST WAY TO STORE FRESH HERBS?

It depends on the herb! Think of parsley, cilantro and mint like bouquets of fresh flowers. Trim the stems, place them in a glass of water, and store them in the refrigerator. Do the same for basil, but keep it on the counter and cover it loosely with a plastic bag. Change the water when it gets low and/or turns murky. Wrap chives, dill, rosemary and thyme in damp paper towels and place in sealed containers in the refrigerator. Your herbs should stay fresh for at least a week!

SAVORY HERB BUTTER

Mixing fresh herbs into vegan butter is a great way to show them off and also to take butter to a whole new level. Each variation features a different herb complemented by aromatics that bring out its essence. But, think about your favorite herbs, play around with the flavors and see what fun combinations you can come up with. How about mint and lemon zest, dill and garlic, and cilantro and lime zest? The possibilities are endless. Really, anything goes!

Place all of the ingredients in a small bowl. Use a silicone spatula to mix well, until all of the herbs and aromatics are evenly distributed.

Scoop the butter into a small bowl or ramekin and cover with plastic wrap.

Alternatively, turn out the butter onto a piece of plastic wrap, roll it, forming a log, and wrap it like a piece of candy.

Chill until firm, at least 30 minutes, before serving.

Store the butter in an airtight container in the refrigerator for up to 1 week or in the freezer for up to 3 months.

Makes approximately
½ cup (114 g) each

CHIVE-PARSLEY-LEMON BUTTER

⅓ cup (75 g) unsalted vegan butter, softened

2 tbsp (6 g) minced fresh chives

1 tbsp (4 g) minced fresh parsley

1 tbsp (6 g) lemon zest

Pinch of salt

SHALLOT-THYME BUTTER

⅓ cup (75 g) unsalted vegan butter, softened

1 tbsp (2 g) minced fresh thyme leaves

1 tbsp (10 g) finely minced shallots

1 tsp lemon zest

Pinch of salt

SUN-DRIED TOMATO-BASIL BUTTER

⅓ cup (75 g) unsalted vegan butter, softened

2 tbsp (30 g) finely chopped and drained sun-dried tomatoes

2 tbsp (5 g) minced fresh basil

Pinch of salt

8 oz (227 g) plain vegan chocolate, finely chopped, divided

2 tbsp (2 g) crushed-up freeze-dried strawberries

1 tsp finely chopped fresh rosemary

Sea salt flakes, a few pinches

ROSEMARY-CHOCOLATE BARK

I am in love with this dessert. It's like a piece of art, with chocolate as the canvas and freeze-dried fruit and herbs as the paint. Not only is it colorful and impressive, especially around the holidays, but chocolate and herbs together are an exceptionally unique pairing.

In this version, sweet strawberries and assertive rosemary are the stars of the show, but there are other combinations you can try, like basil and strawberries, mint and orange zest, dill and lemon zest, thyme and blueberries, and even cilantro with bananas and lime zest. No matter which combination you choose, tap into your inner artist to create your own dessert masterpiece.

Line a quarter sheet pan with parchment paper and set a folded kitchen towel on the counter. Make room in the refrigerator for the sheet pan to sit flat.

Bring a small pot of water to a boil. Set a heatproof bowl over the boiling water and add two-thirds of the chocolate. Do not stir as the chocolate begins to melt.

When about three-quarters of the chocolate has melted, lift the bowl off the pot, turn off the heat and place the bowl on the kitchen towel. Add the remaining chocolate and gently stir until all of the chocolate is melted.

Pour the chocolate onto the sheet pan. Use an offset spatula to spread it out evenly, almost to the edges.

Working quickly, sprinkle the freeze-dried strawberries, rosemary and sea salt over the surface of the chocolate.

Place the bark in the refrigerator to set, at least 1 hour.

When ready to serve, break the bark into uneven shards.

INDIAN BLACK SALT

Indian black salt has exactly one job in a vegan kitchen: to make things taste like eggs. This is not an egg replacer in the style of aquafaba or flaxseed. This is a condiment that literally tastes like eggs.

Indian black salt is also called Himalayan salt or kala namak. It's a naturally occurring volcanic rock salt found in the salt mines of India, Pakistan and Nepal. It was discovered thousands of years ago and was originally used in Ayurvedic medicine.

The salt is heated to extremely high temperatures and mixed with herbs and spices. Because it's naturally high in sulfur, the end result is a salt that is pinkish in color and tastes pungent, savory and sulfuric, basically like hard-boiled eggs.

Try it. Mash some garbanzo beans or crumble some tofu in a bowl. Add Five-Minute Mayo (page 15), diced celery, fresh dill, a hit of mustard and a big pinch of Indian black salt. Mix it all together and voilà! You've got an egg salad facsimile. Now you know what I'm talking about.

If that makes you do a happy dance, try making The Breakfast Sandwich (page 65). A slab of tofu is seasoned with Indian black salt and piled into a sandwich that rivals anything you can get at the corner bodega. In the mood for an omelet? Add Indian black salt to garbanzo bean flour and you've got eggy Mushroom Omelets (page 66). Or take your avocado toast to the next level with eggy scrambled tofu in Avocado Toast with Eggy Tofu Scram and Quick Pickles (page 69).

This is why Indian black salt is a must-have in a vegan kitchen. Look for it in South Asian markets or order it online. It's inexpensive and a little goes a long way, so you won't have to replace your stash very often.

THE BREAKFAST SANDWICH

Makes 2

The breakfast sandwich is kind of an institution in New York City, so if you are going to make a vegan one, it has to be good enough to rival the best of them. A thick slab of tofu is seasoned with Indian black salt and a little turmeric (for color; it has to be yellow!), then it's piled onto English muffins and topped with tamari-roasted red onions and massaged kale. It's healthy, satisfying and delicious.

Preheat the oven to 350°F (177°C). Line a half sheet pan with parchment paper.

To prepare the tofu, brush the top, bottom and sides with olive oil. Lightly shake the turmeric over the tofu and use your fingers to rub it into the tofu on all sides. Sprinkle a big pinch of Indian black salt over the top of each piece and rub it in. Place it on one side of the sheet pan.

To prepare the onions, whisk together the olive oil and tamari. Drizzle it over the onions and toss to coat. Place them on the other half of the sheet pan.

Place the sheet pan in the oven and bake for 30 minutes.

In the meantime, prepare the kale. Place the kale in a big mixing bowl. Add the lime juice and salt. Get in there with both hands and massage the kale until the leaves become tender and reduce down in size, about 1 minute.

When the tofu and onions are ready, toast the English muffins.

To assemble the sandwiches, butter both sides of the English muffins. Divide the kale and pile it on the bottom half. Layer with a piece of tofu and top each one with half of the roasted onions. Top with the other half of the English muffin.

TOFU

7.5 oz (225 g) extra-firm tofu (½ standard block), drained and cut into 2 rectangles

2 tsp (10 ml) good olive oil

Turmeric, a few shakes

Indian black salt, a few pinches

TAMARI-ROASTED RED ONIONS

1 tbsp (15 ml) good olive oil

1 tbsp (15 ml) tamari

1 red onion, cut into rings

MASSAGED KALE

2 leaves curly kale

1 tbsp (15 ml) fresh lime juice

Pinch of salt

TO SERVE

2 English muffins

Sun-Dried Tomato–Basil Butter (page 59)

MUSHROOM FILLING

1 tsp good olive oil

1 shallot, thinly sliced

1 clove of garlic, pressed

2 baby bella mushrooms, thinly sliced

1 sprig fresh thyme

¼ tsp Indian black salt

OMELET

¼ cup (30 g) garbanzo bean flour

1 tbsp (8 g) arrowroot starch/flour

½ tsp Indian black salt

¼ tsp baking soda

¼ cup (60 ml) plus 1 tbsp (15 ml) plain unsweetened soy milk

½ tsp ume plum vinegar

Vegan butter, for cooking

TO SERVE

Fresh chives, finely chopped

MUSHROOM OMELETS

You know those omelet stations they have at hotels or fancy brunch parties? Well, you can have a plant-based one at home! The omelet base is made with garbanzo bean flour that is seasoned with Indian black salt into a batter that stands in as a facsimile for eggs. Fill it with whatever you love in an omelet, like sautéed baby bellas, shallots and fresh thyme. Once you have perfected the omelet making and folding part, you can really go in any direction you want.

To prepare the filling, heat the olive oil in a cast-iron or nonstick skillet over low heat. When it's shimmering, add the shallots and garlic. Cook until the shallots become translucent and the garlic is fragrant, about 8 minutes.

Turn the heat up to medium and add the mushrooms. Toss to coat the mushrooms with the shallot-garlic-oil mixture and cook, until the mushrooms start to turn golden brown, about 7 minutes. Pull the thyme leaves from the sprig and add them to the mixture. Add the Indian black salt and mix to combine.

In the meantime, make the omelet batter. Add the garbanzo bean flour, arrowroot, Indian black salt and baking soda to a small bowl. Whisk to combine. Add the soy milk and ume plum vinegar. Whisk together until completely smooth.

Heat a cast-iron griddle or nonstick skillet over medium-low heat and add a dollop of butter. As it sizzles, use a spatula to coat the entire pan. Pour the omelet batter into the pan in a nice thin circle. Cook for about 3 to 4 minutes, until the top starts to bubble and look dry. Carefully loosen up the omelet with a spatula and flip it over. Cook for another 2 to 3 minutes.

Lift the omelet out of the pan and onto a plate. Add the mushroom mixture to one side and fold the other half of the omelet over the top. Sprinkle with chives.

AVOCADO TOAST WITH EGGY TOFU SCRAM AND QUICK PICKLES

Avocado on toast is a thing. Topped with scrambled tofu that has been seasoned with Indian black salt and nutritional yeast, it's an even better thing. But wait. Can that buttery, eggy, slightly cheesy bite of deliciousness get even better? Yes! Top with Quick Pickles (page 152) for a crunchy, vinegary kick.

Heat a skillet over medium heat. Add the olive oil. When it's shimmering, add the turmeric. Use a wooden spoon with a flat edge to stir the turmeric into the oil.

Crumble the tofu and add it to the skillet. Mix the tofu into the turmeric. Add the nutritional yeast and Indian black salt. Mix again and cook until the tofu is scrambled and heated through, about 5 minutes. Take it off the heat and mix in the chives.

Toast the bread. Spread the mashed avocado on the toast and top with the tofu scram. Decorate with the Quick Pickles and season with freshly ground black pepper.

1 tbsp (15 ml) good olive oil

¼ tsp turmeric

7.5 oz (225 g) firm tofu (½ standard block), drained

1 tbsp (5 g) nutritional yeast

1 tsp Indian black salt

1 tbsp (3 g) chopped fresh chives

TO SERVE

4 slices of your favorite bread

1 avocado, mashed

Quick Pickles (page 152)

Freshly ground black pepper

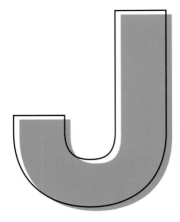

JACKFRUIT

Jackfruit is the fruit of the—you guessed it—tropical jackfruit tree. Grown across South and Southeast Asia, jackfruit trees are quite prolific. Each tree can grow hundreds of fruits and each fruit, which looks like a nubby, gigantic, oblong melon, can weigh up to a hundred pounds. In fact, jackfruit is the largest tree fruit in the world!

While it has risen in popularity in the United States in the last decade, it has been a staple food in Asian cuisine forever. Here is what they know that we didn't know. Young, unripe jackfruit has a mild flavor and a meaty texture. And when jackfruit is shredded, it's reminiscent in color and appearance to shredded white meat. The first time I saw it, I did a double take. Seriously.

From a nutrition perspective, jackfruit contains almost every vitamin and mineral a human being needs, as well as protein, fiber and antioxidants. It's good for digestion, for the immune system and has been shown to boost energy levels. From an environmental perspective, jackfruit is a highly efficient and sustainable crop. So, clearly, we need more jackfruit recipes.

When you are out shopping for jackfruit, look for BPA-free cans in the same aisle you find artichoke hearts or packages near the tempeh and tofu. Even if you are able to find a whole young jackfruit at the market, don't even bother. It's not worth the time and effort it takes to hack through such a big piece of fruit that contains this crazy, sticky sap that gets everywhere and makes the whole thing not very fun.

Look for labels that say plain, young and/or green jackfruit. Sometimes they even say vegetable meat! Jackfruit packed in water is preferable, but if you can only find it packed in brine, that's fine, just give it an extra rinse before you start prepping it.

Jackfruit can be made on the stovetop, cooked down with herbs and spices, or marinated and baked in the oven. Try Without-a-Wok Jackfruit Lo Mein (page 73) if you are in the mood for Chinese, or Jackfruit Tacos al Pastor with Pineapple Salsa (page 74) if you are in the mood for Mexican.

Get to know jackfruit well. Think about all of the recipes you have that call for shredded meat and make the swap. How about seasoning it with barbecue sauce and making pulled jackfruit sliders? Or how about taking the taco meat you made for the al pastor tacos and layering it into Easy Cheesy Loaded Nachos (page 100)? Once you get comfortable with jackfruit, the possibilities are endless!

WHAT IS UMAMI?

Umami is considered the fifth taste, along with sweet, salty, sour and bitter. Umami is a Japanese word that translates to pleasant savory taste and deliciousness and basically explains everything about why we like to eat what we like to eat. It was coined by a Japanese chemist in the early 1900s who discovered that the unique flavor of three specific amino acids, including glutamate, found in certain foods—including meat, seafood and aged cheeses—activates our taste receptors and creates a satisfying, savory flavor experience. But there are plant foods that are also rich in umami, like mushrooms, tomatoes, garlic, olives and fermented foods like miso, tempeh, tamari, umeboshi and vinegar. Umami-rich ingredients are listed in almost every recipe throughout this book because it's what makes your food taste delicious!

WITHOUT-A-WOK JACKFRUIT LO MEIN

Lo mein means "tossed noodles." It's a traditional Chinese dish of noodles tossed with meat, vegetables and brown sauce. I used to love ordering it whenever we went out for Chinese food. In this plant-based version, shredded jackfruit is the meat and the vegetables are mushrooms, carrots and bok choy, but they are definitely swappable with your favorites.

Use any noodles you like. I like thick Chinese noodles like yakisoba, but thin noodles, rice noodles, ramen noodles and even spaghetti all work great. And, you don't need a wok to make this lo mein. A wide shallow pan works just fine.

Bring a big pot of salted water to a boil and cook the noodles according to the package instructions. Drain and set aside.

To prepare the jackfruit, cut off the hard cores, remove any seeds and seed pods and discard. Shred the rest, leaving some chunkier pieces. Set aside.

Heat a wide shallow pan or Dutch oven over medium heat. Add the sunflower oil. When it's shimmering, add the onions and cook until translucent, about 5 minutes. Add the garlic and ginger. Cook until the garlic and ginger are fragrant, about 1 minute.

Add the jackfruit and water and use tongs to mix around. Cook with the cover askew, until most of the water is absorbed, about 10 to 12 minutes.

Add the mushrooms. Stir them into the jackfruit and onion mixture and cook, until the mushrooms start to turn golden brown, about 7 minutes. Season with salt and pepper.

Add the carrots and bok choy. Cook until the bok choy is wilted and bright green, about 3 to 5 minutes. Add the noodles and toss everything together.

In the meantime, prepare the sauce. Add the water, tamari, umeboshi paste, miso and mirin to a small mixing bowl. Break up the miso with a small silicone spatula and whisk the sauce together until completely smooth.

Pour the sauce over the top and use tongs to mix it until everything is fully coated.

Serve topped with scallions.

NOODLES

½ lb (227 g) uncooked thick Chinese noodles

JACKFRUIT AND VEGETABLES

1 (14-oz [397-g]) can young jackfruit, drained and rinsed

1 tbsp (15 ml) sunflower oil

1 small onion, cut into half-moons

2 cloves garlic, pressed

1 tbsp (15 g) grated fresh ginger

¼ cup (60 ml) water

6 baby bella mushrooms, thinly sliced

Pinch of salt

Dash of pepper

2 carrots, shredded

1 big or 2 baby bok choy, cut into ¼-inch (6-mm) pieces

SAUCE

¼ cup (60 ml) water

2 tbsp (30 ml) tamari

2 tbsp (36 g) umeboshi paste

2 tsp (10 ml) mellow white miso

1 tbsp (15 ml) mirin

TO SERVE

2 scallions, white and green parts, thinly sliced

Makes 8

JACKFRUIT TACOS AL PASTOR WITH PINEAPPLE SALSA

Tacos al pastor are tacos "in the style of the shepherd." Lebanese immigrants brought their style of cooking meat on a vertical skewer to Mexico and, eventually, it was adopted by the locals to create a flavorful filling for tacos. In this rendition, jackfruit is shredded and marinated in pineapple and orange juice and traditional Mexican spices, baked and served topped with pineapple salsa. Make these tacos on Taco Tuesday or any day of the week!

JACKFRUIT

2 (14-oz [397-g]) cans young jackfruit, drained and rinsed

¼ cup (60 ml) pineapple juice (reserved from the can you will use for the salsa)

¼ cup (60 ml) orange juice

1 tbsp (15 ml) apple cider vinegar

1 tsp chipotle chili powder

1 tsp Mexican oregano

1 tsp cumin

1 tsp garlic powder

1 tsp onion powder

Pinch of salt

PINEAPPLE SALSA

1 (15-oz [425-g]) can pineapple, diced

¼ cup (40 g) diced red onion

1 jalapeño, seeds and ribs removed, diced

2 tbsp (2 g) chopped fresh cilantro

2 tbsp (3 g) chopped fresh mint

1 tbsp (12 g) lime zest

2 tbsp (30 ml) fresh lime juice

Pinch of salt

TO SERVE

8 corn tortillas

Pickled Jalapeños (page 152)

Toasted pumpkin seeds

Lime wedges

To prepare the jackfruit, cut off the hard cores, remove any seeds and seed pods and discard. Shred the rest and set aside.

In a big mixing bowl, whisk together the pineapple juice, orange juice, apple cider vinegar, chipotle chili powder, oregano, cumin, garlic powder, onion powder and salt.

Add the jackfruit to the marinade and toss to coat well. Marinate for 30 minutes.

Preheat the oven to 350°F (177°C). Line a half sheet pan with parchment paper.

Use a slotted spoon to lift the jackfruit out of the marinade and arrange it in a single layer on the sheet pan. Discard any leftover marinade. Bake for 35 to 40 minutes, until the jackfruit is brown and dry.

In the meantime, prepare the salsa. Add the pineapple, onions, jalapeño, cilantro, mint, lime zest, lime juice and salt to a small mixing bowl. Mix well and set aside.

To prepare the tortillas, char them one at a time on an open flame or heat them on a dry cast-iron skillet.

To assemble the tacos, layer with jackfruit and top with pineapple salsa, Pickled Jalapeños and pumpkin seeds. Serve with lime wedges.

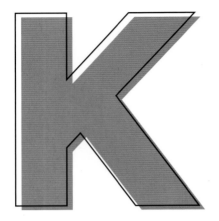

KALE

You have to eat kale if you are vegan. It's mandatory. Just kidding! Not really.

Kale is one of the most nutrient-dense foods on planet Earth. It's packed with vitamins A, B, C (more than an orange!) and K. It's high in fiber and low in fat. It also has tons of minerals, including calcium, potassium, magnesium and iron. It's good for heart and brain health, skin and hair health, and eye and bone health. It's an energy booster and an anti-inflammatory.

So, yes, you have to eat kale. The thing is, kale can be hard to love. It's bitter. It's tough. It's chewy. But if you work on it, kale can be very enjoyable, tender, sweet even and quite delicious. Once you know how to use which kale in what dish, you will start to love it and—dare I say—even crave it?

When you are out shopping for kale, you will encounter several varieties. No matter which you choose, always look for kale that is vibrantly green (not yellow) with crisp leaves and firm and healthy stems.

Curly kale is probably the most common variety you will see at the market. It's bright or dark green (and sometimes has purple veining) with frilly edges and long stems. Curly kale is a little peppery and slightly bitter and best when eaten raw, which makes it a great choice for smoothies and salads.

But, remember how I said that raw kale is hard to love? To make it more palatable, massage it! I know, it sounds weird, but working the kale with some acid, like lemon juice or vinegar, breaks down the tough fibers and softens up the leaves. Trust me, it turned me from a kale hater into a kale lover. Check out The Big Kale Salad with Seedy Sprinkle Cheese (page 79) and Easy Cheesy Loaded Nachos (page 100).

Tuscan kale—also known as dinosaur and lacinato—has flat, dark bluish-greenish leaves that are kind of crinkled and scaly. It's hearty and sweet in a vegetable kind of way and really shines in cooked dishes.

To get an idea, heat a little bit of good olive oil in a big cast-iron or nonstick skillet, add some pressed garlic and crushed red pepper flakes, and sauté for a minute. Add coarsely chopped Tuscan kale and toss it around until it's wilted and soft. Season it with salt and fresh lemon juice and you will fall in love with how tender it is. Or make Tuscan Kale and White Bean Soup (page 80) and see how stewing kale for a while breaks it down even more into a silky soft, flavorful version of itself.

And then there is baby kale, the young immature leaves of the kale plant. Baby kale is super tender and very mild in flavor. You can sometimes find baby kale loose at the market, but you will definitely find it by the packaged salad greens. It's delicate like spinach and peppery like arugula and can be used interchangeably.

Baby kale doesn't need any doctoring to taste great. It wilts down in seconds and adds a little greenery and nutrition to dishes like The Breakfast Sandwich (page 65), Millet-Corn Salad with Baby Kale and Garlic-Chive Vinaigrette (page 160) and Green Beans and Baby Kale with XO Sauce (page 168).

THE BIG KALE SALAD WITH SEEDY SPRINKLE CHEESE

Serves 2

A big kale salad starts with, you guessed it, a pile of curly kale! Remember: Massaging the kale breaks down the tough fibers and softens up the leaves so you end up with the perfect texture and flavor. Because kale is so hearty, you can do this a few hours ahead of time and it won't even get close to wilted!

To make this salad a complete meal, add all of the delicious things like protein-rich quinoa and garbanzo beans, colorful tomatoes, sweet corn, chewy raisins, briny green olives and fresh chives. Dress it with White Balsamic Vinaigrette (page 155) and top it all off with Seedy Sprinkle Cheese, a fantastic plant-based Parmesan that is made with three of our star ingredients—sunflower seeds, hemp seeds and nutritional yeast.

To make the seedy sprinkle cheese, heat a cast-iron or nonstick skillet over low heat. Add the hemp seeds and toast, stirring around occasionally, until they start to brown just slightly, about 5 minutes. Let cool.

Add the toasted hemp seeds, sunflower seeds, nutritional yeast, miso and onion powder to the bowl of a small food processor. Pulse a few times until the mixture is crumbly and combined. Store in an airtight container in the refrigerator.

Place the kale in a big mixing bowl. Add the lemon juice and salt. Get in there with both hands and massage the kale until the leaves become tender and reduce in size, about 1 minute.

Add the quinoa, garbanzo beans, tomatoes, corn, raisins, olives, chives, sunflower seeds and hemp seeds.

Add as much vinaigrette as you like and toss to coat. Top with seedy sprinkle cheese.

SEEDY SPRINKLE CHEESE

½ cup (80 g) hemp seeds

½ cup (67 g) toasted sunflower seeds

¼ cup (20 g) nutritional yeast

1 tbsp (15 ml) mellow white miso

1 tsp onion powder

KALE SALAD

1 bunch curly kale, destemmed and chopped into bite-size pieces

2 tbsp (30 ml) fresh lemon juice

Salt, a couple pinches, divided

½ cup (93 g) cooked quinoa

½ cup (82 g) cooked garbanzo beans

½ cup (75 g) mixed cherry or grape tomatoes, halved

½ cup (77 g) sweet corn

¼ cup (36 g) golden raisins

¼ cup (45 g) pitted green olives, thinly sliced

2 tbsp (6 g) chopped fresh chives

2 tbsp (16 g) toasted sunflower seeds

1 tbsp (10 g) hemp seeds

TO SERVE

White Balsamic Vinaigrette (page 155)

Serves 4

1 tbsp (15 ml) good olive oil

1 small onion, diced

2 carrots, cut into rounds

1 rib celery, diced

2 cloves garlic

1 tsp dried oregano

1 tsp crushed red pepper

Pinch of salt

Dash of pepper

¼ cup (66 g) tomato paste

1 bunch Tuscan kale, destemmed and cut into thick strips

1½ cups (246 g) cooked or 1 (15-oz [425-g]) can white beans, drained

3 cups (720 ml) water

3 sprigs fresh thyme

1 bay leaf

1 tsp sherry vinegar

TO SERVE

Seedy Sprinkle Cheese (page 79)

TUSCAN KALE AND WHITE BEAN SOUP

This hearty soup originated in Tuscany and is an easy, one-pot meal. Use your favorite white beans. Cannellini, white kidney, Great Northern and mayocoba beans all work well. No matter which you choose, they are just there to support the star of the show: luscious, silky Tuscan kale. It may seem like a lot of kale at first, but it cooks down significantly. Serve this soup with crusty bread because you will need something to wipe out the bottom of the bowl!

Heat a heavy-bottomed soup pot over medium heat. Add the olive oil. When it's shimmering, add the onions, carrots and celery and cook until the vegetables start to soften, about 10 minutes. Add the garlic, oregano, crushed red pepper, salt and pepper; mix around and cook until the garlic is fragrant, about 1 minute.

Add the tomato paste and use a wooden spoon to mix it around, cooking it for 3 to 4 minutes.

Add the kale, white beans and water and stir around. Add the thyme and bay leaf. Bring to a boil, reduce to a simmer and cook with the cover askew for 15 minutes, until the kale is completely wilted and soft.

Remove the thyme sprigs and bay leaf and stir in the sherry vinegar.

Serve topped with Seedy Sprinkle Cheese.

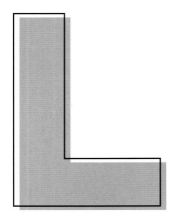

LENTILS

Lentils have been a source of sustenance since ancient times. Thought to have originated in the Mediterranean, lentils are the oldest pulse crop known to man and one of the earliest domesticated crops. Like dates, they make an appearance in the Bible. In the book of Genesis, Esau sold his birthright to his brother Jacob for "some bread and some lentil stew." That must have been some really good stew!

Lentils are inexpensive, have a long shelf life, are easy to make and are very nutritious. They are low in fat, low in calories, high in protein and high in soluble fiber. They are packed with iron, B vitamins, magnesium, zinc, selenium and potassium.

It's hard to describe exactly what lentils taste like. They are earthy in a way that is reminiscent of fresh soil after a light rain, but in a good way. They taste pleasant and familiar and come in a variety of colors, all the way from light yellow to deep black. The darker the lentils, the more intense their flavor, which totally makes sense.

When you think of lentils, if you think of them at all, you probably picture green or brown lentils, the lentils of lentil soup. They can be used interchangeably but green lentils have an almost peppery flavor, while brown lentils have a milder, more neutral flavor. They both cook quickly, hold their shape very well and are most often used in soups and stews like Potato and Two-Lentil Stew (page 85).

Red and yellow lentils are really mild, bright and almost sweet. They totally lose their shape when cooked down. Actually, they become total mush, which is kind of their point. They are a vehicle to showcase bold flavors, to add texture and to thicken curries, stews and soups. In fact, they are the secret to the aforementioned stew.

French lentils, also known as puy lentils, are a really pretty greenish-bluish-gray color with little speckles. Black lentils, also known as beluga lentils, are little, round and black. When cooked, they both hold their shape really well and are great options for this gorgeous Lentil Salad with Roasted Beets and Fresh Herbs (page 86).

Lentils are a super-versatile ingredient and are worth getting to know. Add them to your favorite chili, mix them up with caramelized onions and fresh herbs or serve them with a platter of your favorite roasted vegetables. You can even toss cooked lentils with taco seasonings (there are two different recipes in this book!) and use them as a fun plant-based taco meat. No matter how you use them, they will always bring a little pop of earthy freshness and a whole lot of health to your meals.

POTATO AND TWO-LENTIL STEW

This stew is comforting and delicious and a great way to get to know lentils. I call for not one, but two different kinds of lentils—hearty brown lentils and creamy red lentils. There is some heat from a generous amount of crushed red pepper and plenty of umami from tomato paste and nutritional yeast. It's so good, it may even entice someone to sell you something (wink, wink). Make it any time of year when you are in the mood for a nourishing bowl of goodness.

Heat a heavy-bottomed soup pot over medium heat. Add the olive oil. When it's shimmering, add the onions, carrots and celery and cook until the vegetables start to soften, about 10 minutes. Add the garlic, crushed red pepper and salt. Cook until the garlic is fragrant, about 1 minute.

Add the tomato paste and use a wooden spoon to mix it around, cooking it for 3 to 4 minutes. Add the nutritional yeast and stir it into the vegetables.

Add the potatoes, brown lentils and red lentils and stir to coat. Add the water and bay leaf and season with another pinch of salt. Bring to a boil, reduce to a simmer and cook with the cover askew for 25 to 30 minutes, stirring occasionally, until the lentils and potatoes are nice and soft. Add more water, 1 cup (240 ml) at a time, if the soup gets too thick.

Remove the bay leaf and stir in the sherry vinegar. Serve topped with parsley.

1 tbsp (15 ml) good olive oil

1 small onion, diced

2 carrots, cut into rounds

1 rib celery, diced

2 cloves garlic, pressed

1 tsp crushed red pepper

Salt, a couple pinches, divided

2 tbsp (32 g) tomato paste

2 tbsp (10 g) nutritional yeast

8 small yellow and/or red potatoes, cut into rounds

¾ cup (144 g) uncooked brown lentils, sorted and rinsed

¼ cup (48 g) uncooked red lentils, sorted and rinsed

3 cups (720 ml) water, or more, if necessary

1 bay leaf

1 tsp sherry vinegar

TO SERVE
Fresh parsley, chopped

LENTIL SALAD WITH ROASTED BEETS AND FRESH HERBS

Serves 4 to 6

I love the look of this dark, moody salad. Beet wedges are seasoned and roasted to bring out their sweetness and paired with dark earthy lentils, crispy cucumbers and fresh bright herbs. All of the different shapes, sizes and textures are really stunning together, not to mention delicious.

4 small beets, peeled and cut into wedges, quarters or eighths, depending on size

1 tbsp (15 ml) good olive oil

Pinch of salt

Dash of pepper

1 cup (192 g) uncooked black or French lentils, sorted and rinsed

1 bay leaf

2 Persian cucumbers, thinly sliced

½ cup (69 g) toasted pumpkin seeds

1 tbsp (3 g) chopped fresh chives

1 tbsp (4 g) chopped fresh parsley

1 tbsp (3 g) chopped fresh dill

1 tbsp (6 g) chopped fresh mint

TO SERVE

Sherry-Shallot Vinaigrette (page 155)

Preheat the oven to 400°F (204°C). Line a sheet pan with parchment paper. Toss the beet wedges with the olive oil, salt and pepper and roast until tender, about 30 to 35 minutes.

In the meantime, prepare the lentils. Add the lentils to a pot and cover with water. Add the bay leaf and cook until tender, but still al dente, about 12 to 15 minutes. Remove the bay leaf, drain and turn out into a big mixing bowl.

Add the beets, cucumbers, pumpkin seeds, chives, parsley, dill and mint to the lentils. Add as much vinaigrette as you like and toss to coat.

Serve warm or at room temperature.

MISO

Miso is a very old, very traditional Japanese condiment. According to Japanese mythology, miso was a gift to mankind from the gods to ensure health, longevity and happiness. I totally believe that, but also in real life, it was invented in China and brought to Japan by Buddhist monks in the 7th century. Over time, the fermented mixture of salt, rice, grains and soybeans evolved into the paste we know today.

Miso is a staple of vegan cooking because it's rich in umami. There are many ways to describe it: funky, savory, sweet, salty, earthy and nutty. There is no exact Western equivalent of miso and not that many other ingredients can add the kind of depth and complexity that miso brings to a dish.

Miso making is considered an art form, a religion almost, a process that was developed over centuries. Cooked beans, usually soybeans, are mixed together with salt and a fermented grain called koji, which is made from rice or barley, and fermented for as little as 3 weeks to as long as 3 years.

There are whole books on fermentation because it's a pretty fascinating process, but basically everything breaks down and transforms. Starches convert to sugar (sweet!). Proteins break down into amino acids (glutamates = umami!). Salt prohibits bad bacteria from forming (salt!). In the end? Miso perfection!

The longer the miso ferments, the deeper the flavor and the darker the color. Generally speaking, there are two basic types of miso: white and red. White miso ferments for the shortest time, is light beige to yellow to an almost peanut buttery color and is sweet and mild. Red miso ferments the longest, is a deep amber to reddish brown color and is the most savory and assertive. Of course, there is a wide range of flavor and color depending on the brand, so do some research and try a few different types to figure out which one you like best.

To get an idea of the depth of flavor and richness of miso, make miso butter. Add ⅓ cup (75 g) of room-temperature vegan butter and 1 tablespoon (15 ml) of miso to a small bowl and use a silicone spatula to mix them together well, until the miso is distributed evenly. Chill it until it's firm, at least 30 minutes. Spread it on a piece of toast or toss it with some noodles or freshly made gnocchi (page 11). See? That's what I'm talking about! It's also a yummy addition to Five-Minute Mayo (page 15).

Think of miso as an all-purpose, salty, deeply umami seasoning that can be used in savory and sweet recipes. Use it to season the broth in Better-Than-Instant Miso Ramen (page 91), marinate tempeh in Miso-Mustard Tempeh with Roasted Baby Bok Choy (page 92) and Miso Eggplant (page 37) and add umami to the sauces for Classic Crusty Mac and Cheese (page 103) and Without-a-Wok Jackfruit Lo Mein (page 73). And, it's the X factor in this spectacular Sweet Buttery Miso Caramel (page 95).

BETTER-THAN-INSTANT MISO RAMEN

Serves 2

I remember the first time I saw someone eating curly ramen noodles out of a Sty-rofoam cup. You know what I am talking about, right? They are called Cup Noodles and were invented by Momofuku Ando, the founder and chairman of Nissin Foods. He started a global revolution, for sure, but why buy a cup of instant noodles when you can make a healthy, homemade version yourself?

This version is inspired by Hokkaido-style ramen. The broth is simple and flavorful and a great way to showcase miso. You will definitely need a spoon and chopsticks to eat this bowl of goodness. Earthy mushrooms and sweet corn are my favorite toppings, but get creative and don't forget the noodles. They are the best part! Speaking of noodles, try to find ramen made with clean ingredients and nothing artificial. If they come with a sauce packet, toss it.

RAMEN NOODLES

2 bunches ramen noodles

MISO BROTH

1½ cups (360 ml) water

1½ tbsp (23 ml) mellow white miso

1 tbsp (15 ml) tamari

1 scallion, white and green parts, thinly sliced

SAUTÉED MUSHROOMS

1 tbsp (15 ml) sunflower oil

8 oz (227 g) baby bella mushrooms, cut in half, quarters or kept whole, if small

Pinch of salt

Dash of pepper

OTHER TOPPINGS

1½ cups (231 g) sweet corn

2 tbsp (6 g) chopped fresh chives

2 tsp (4 g) toasted sesame seeds

Bring a big pot of salted water to a boil and cook the ramen noodles according to the package instructions. Drain and set aside.

In the meantime, prepare the miso broth. Add the water, miso and tamari to a small saucepan. Bring to a high simmer and whisk vigorously to dissolve the miso. Turn the heat to low, add the scallions and let it sit to keep the broth warm.

To prepare the mushrooms, heat the sunflower oil in a cast-iron or nonstick skillet over low heat. When it's shimmering, add the mushrooms. Toss to coat with the oil and cook, until the mushrooms start to turn golden brown, about 7 minutes. Season with salt and pepper.

To assemble, divide the noodles between two bowls. Arrange the mushrooms and corn on top of the noodles. Whisk the broth and ladle half into each bowl. Top with chives and sesame seeds.

Serves 2

ROASTED BABY BOK CHOY

2 tsp (10 ml) sunflower oil

2 tsp (10 ml) tamari

4 baby bok choy, cut in half, lengthwise

MISO-MUSTARD TEMPEH

1 (8-oz [227-g]) package soy tempeh, cut into 8 rectangles

1 tbsp (15 ml) mellow white miso

1 tbsp (15 ml) water

1 tbsp (15 ml) grainy mustard

1 tbsp (15 ml) tamari

1 tbsp (15 ml) sunflower oil

TO SERVE

Fresh lemon juice

Toasted sesame seeds

MISO-MUSTARD TEMPEH WITH ROASTED BABY BOK CHOY

This marinade is one of my all-time favorite combinations. The spicy mustard and the savory miso perfectly complement the earthy nuttiness of the tempeh. With tender stems and crispy leaves, the roasted bok choy is special in its own right. Squeeze fresh lemon juice over the top right before you are about to eat to bring out the best in every flavor. Altogether, this plate is not only healthy but pretty too! Serve with a nice little bowl of rice or quinoa for a complete meal.

Preheat the oven to 400°F (204°C). Line a quarter sheet pan with parchment paper.

To prepare the bok choy, whisk together the sunflower oil and tamari in a small mixing bowl. Place the bok choy on the sheet pan, cut side up. Drizzle the oil and tamari mixture over the top of the bok choy as evenly as you can.

Place the bok choy in the oven and roast for 10 minutes. Take them out, turn them over so they are now cut side down and bake for another 5 to 10 minutes, until the leaves are charred.

At the same time, prepare the tempeh. Add the tempeh to a pan with sides and cover with water. Bring to a boil, reduce to a simmer and cook, uncovered, for 10 minutes.

Add the miso, water, mustard, tamari and sunflower oil to a big mixing bowl. Break up the miso with a small silicone spatula and then whisk the marinade together until completely smooth.

When the tempeh has finished simmering, drain it and drop it into the marinade, flipping it over to coat both sides. Marinate for 10 minutes.

Heat a cast-iron or nonstick skillet over medium heat. Add the tempeh and cook until the first side starts to brown and the marinade dries up a bit, about 5 minutes. Flip the tempeh over and cook the second side, until it starts to brown, another 5 minutes.

Serve with a drizzle of lemon juice and a sprinkle of sesame seeds.

SWEET BUTTERY MISO CARAMEL

Vegan caramel is not only possible, it's delicious. It's made the same way as traditional caramel but with coconut milk and miso. The result? A lightly colored, luxurious, buttery sweet and salty caramel. Use it anywhere you would normally use caramel, like drizzled over apples, spooned over vegan ice cream or, for a really fun treat, drizzled over Cheesy Popcorn (page 104). But if you really want to impress people with it, make a Banana-Caramel Upside-Down Cake (page 45).

Add the sugar and water to a small saucepan and stir to combine. Turn the heat on medium-low and cook, without stirring, but swirling the pot occasionally, until the mixture is bubbly and has turned a light amber color, about 8 to 10 minutes. Take the pan off the heat and set aside.

In the meantime, add the coconut milk, miso, butter and salt to a separate small saucepan. Use a small silicone spatula to break up the miso. Turn the heat on low and whisk to work the miso into the coconut milk and butter, until the mixture is completely smooth and warm.

Slowly pour the warm coconut milk–miso–butter mixture into the sugar and quickly whisk it together. Be careful; it will bubble up and will be wicked hot. Cover and let cool.

If not using immediately, store in an airtight container in the refrigerator for up to 3 days or in the freezer for up to 3 months. Bring to room temperature before using.

Makes approximately
1 cup (240 ml)

1 cup (192 g) vegan cane sugar

¼ cup (60 ml) cold water

½ cup (120 ml) reduced-fat unsweetened coconut milk

2 tbsp (30 ml) mellow white miso

2 tsp (10 g) vegan butter

Pinch of salt

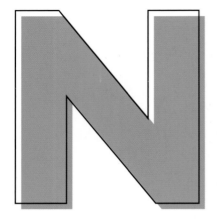

NUTRITIONAL YEAST

Nutritional yeast is a must-have in your vegan pantry. I am not sure how it got such a boring name. Everyone calls it "nooch" for short, but the name is here to stay, so let's figure it out.

First, nutrition. Nutritional yeast is a complete protein, meaning that it contains all nine essential amino acids, making it an excellent plant-based protein source. It contains trace minerals like iron and selenium and powerful antioxidants that protect cells from damage caused by free radicals and heavy metals. And nutritional yeast is usually fortified with B12, a nutrient that is not naturally found in plants, but important for optimal health.

Now, yeast. Nutritional yeast is a unique strain of yeast. It's grown on a medium, like molasses or sugar cane, for several days. When it's ready, it's harvested, heated and deactivated. Then, it's washed, dried, flaked (it kinda sorta looks like fish food!) and packaged up so we can buy tons of it to make all kinds of things. (But not bread or beer. You need live active yeast to make those.)

See? Nutritional. Yeast. Nutritional yeast! Now that we have cleared that up, why is nutritional yeast an essential ingredient in a plant-based kitchen? Because it tastes like cheese!

Disclaimer!! I know that making things taste cheesy is not the same thing as dairy cheese. But, in a vegan kitchen, cheesy means making food that is meant to be reminiscent of, but not exactly like, the original.

Not only does nutritional yeast taste cheesy, but it also adds a salty, nutty, savory layer of flavor to your food. In other words, it's an umami bomb, and all it takes is a tablespoon or two to get the full cheesy effect. Try it! Sprinkle it over steamed vegetables, mix it into vegan mashed potatoes or toss it with noodles and vegan butter.

Use it to add extra layers of flavor to dishes like As-Spicy-as-You-Want-It Pasta e Ceci (page 55), Avocado Toast with Eggy Tofu Scram and Quick Pickles (page 69), Potato and Two-Lentil Stew (page 85), Vegetable Jambalaya (page 128) and Modern Portobello Stroganoff (page 115). Then make all of the cheesy things like Seedy Sprinkle Cheese (page 79), Easy Cheesy Loaded Nachos (page 100), Classic Crusty Mac and Cheese (page 103) and Cheesy Popcorn (page 104).

Think of nutritional yeast as an all-purpose seasoning. Use it in all of your cheesy plant-based adventures and to create other deeply flavorful dishes.

Serves 4 to 6

NACHO CHEESE SAUCE

1 medium-sized russet potato, peeled and chopped

1 carrot, peeled and chopped

½ white onion, chopped

2 cloves garlic, peeled

2 tbsp (30 ml) reserved cooking liquid, plus more, if necessary

¼ cup (20 g) nutritional yeast

2 tbsp (30 ml) sunflower oil

1 tsp apple cider vinegar

½ tsp garlic powder

½ tsp onion powder

½ tsp mustard powder

¼ tsp chipotle chili powder or chili powder

Pinch of salt

GUACAMOLE

1 avocado

2 tbsp (19 g) diced red onion

1 tbsp (15 ml) fresh lime juice

2 tsp (1 g) chopped fresh cilantro

2 tsp (1 g) chopped fresh mint

Pinch of salt

LIME-MASSAGED KALE

2 leaves curly kale, destemmed and finely chopped

1 tbsp (15 ml) fresh lime juice

Pinch of salt

TO SERVE

1 (8-oz [227-g]) bag tortilla chips, yellow or blue, or a combination

½ cup (120 ml) vegan sour cream

¼ cup (40 g) diced red onion

2 scallions, white and green parts, thinly sliced

Pickled Jalapeños (page 152)

EASY CHEESY LOADED NACHOS

This is an epic platter of goodness that rivals anything you can get at a bar or restaurant. The cheesy nacho sauce is made from potatoes. Yes, potatoes! When they are blended, the starches break down and they come out thick and sticky. This is not good for soup (I learned this years ago in an epic potato soup fail), but it's great for a vegan rendition of nacho sauce. You can even make it ahead of time and store it in an airtight container in the refrigerator for up to 1 week or in the freezer for up to 6 months. It will thicken up, so add it to the blender to whip it back up into creamy deliciousness.

If you like your nacho sauce smoky, use chipotle chili powder. Otherwise, use regular chili powder. Just don't forget the nooch! When you are ready, start piling it on and be sure to arrange it so that you get a little bit of everything in each bite!

To make the nacho cheese sauce, add the potatoes, carrots, onions and garlic to a deep pot. Cover with water, bring to a boil and cook until everything is soft, about 10 to 15 minutes.

Drain the vegetables, reserve a ¼ cup (60 ml) of the cooking liquid and put it back into the pot to cool off for a few minutes.

Add the cooked vegetables, 2 tablespoons (30 ml) of the reserved cooking liquid, nutritional yeast, sunflower oil, apple cider vinegar, garlic powder, onion powder, mustard powder, chipotle chili powder and salt to a blender. Process until the sauce is creamy, scraping down the sides of the blender, as necessary, about 1 to 2 minutes. If the mixture needs help processing, add 1 or 2 tablespoons (15 or 30 ml) of the reserved cooking liquid. Set aside.

To make the guacamole, mash the avocado with a fork in a small mixing bowl. Add the onions, lime juice, cilantro, mint and salt. Mix together. Taste the guacamole and add more of any of the ingredients until you are happy with the flavor.

To make the lime-massaged kale, place the kale in a big mixing bowl. Add the lime juice and salt. Get in there with both hands and massage the kale until the leaves become tender and reduce in size, about 1 minute.

To assemble the nachos, make a single layer of chips on a serving platter or quarter sheet pan. Drizzle with the nacho cheese sauce. Dollop guacamole and sour cream over the sauce. Top with half of the kale, onions, scallions and Pickled Jalapeños. Repeat, making another layer, until you have used up all of the ingredients.

CLASSIC CRUSTY MAC AND CHEESE

Serves 4

It's no small feat to make a tasty, velvety vegan macaroni and cheese. The goal is to make a sauce that is reminiscent of, but not exactly, dairy cheese. In this recipe, it's done by cooking up some aromatics and blending them with coconut milk, lots of nooch and other flavors. The end result is kinda sorta like the stuff that comes in that blue box, but way better and way healthier. And, this sauce is another easy one to make ahead of time. Store it in an airtight container in the refrigerator for up to 3 days or in the freezer for up to 6 months.

I like to serve mac and cheese in individual pot pie bakers, but it tastes just as good all in one big baking dish.

Heat a cast-iron or nonstick skillet over medium-low heat. Add the olive oil and butter and melt them together. Add the onions, shallots and garlic. Cook until the onion and shallots are soft and translucent and the garlic is fragrant, about 8 minutes.

Deglaze the pan with the white wine and cook until the wine is mostly absorbed, about 2 minutes. Transfer to a blender. Add the coconut milk, water, nutritional yeast, roasted red pepper, sun-dried tomatoes, miso, ume plum vinegar and salt. Blend until smooth, about 1 minute or so, depending on your machine, until the sauce is thoroughly smooth and creamy. Set aside.

In the meantime, bring a big pot of salted water to a boil and cook the macaroni according to the package instructions. Drain the macaroni and put it back into the pot. Pour the cheese sauce over the macaroni and mix well.

Turn out the macaroni and cheese mixture into a 1-quart (946-g) baking dish or evenly divide it into four pot pie bakers. Sprinkle with paprika and set under the broiler until the top is crispy, about 5 minutes.

1 tbsp (15 ml) good olive oil

1 tbsp (14 g) vegan butter

1 small onion, coarsely chopped

2 shallots, coarsely chopped

2 cloves garlic, pressed

¼ cup (60 ml) vegan white wine

½ cup (120 ml) reduced-fat unsweetened coconut milk

½ cup (120 ml) water

¼ cup (20 g) nutritional yeast

1 roasted red pepper

2 sun-dried tomatoes or 1 tbsp (16 g) tomato paste

1 tbsp (15 ml) mellow white miso

1 tbsp (15 ml) ume plum vinegar

Pinch of salt

½ lb (226 g) uncooked macaroni

TO SERVE

Paprika, a few shakes

Serves 4

---

1 tbsp (15 ml) melted refined coconut oil

½ cup (96 g) popcorn kernels

4 tbsp (56 g) vegan butter

2 tbsp (10 g) nutritional yeast, plus more to top it off, if desired

1 tsp salt

CHEESY POPCORN

Not only is popcorn fun to eat, but it's super healthy. Corn is another whole grain that is rich in vitamins, minerals and antioxidants and is one of the world's best sources of fiber. It's good for heart health, digestive health and reduces the risk of developing many diseases. So how can it get any better? With a hit of nooch! It's called "cheesy" popcorn for a reason!

Add the coconut oil to a deep pot that has a cover. Add the popcorn kernels and shake to distribute them across the bottom of the pot. Cover the pot and turn the heat to medium. The kernels will start to pop in a few minutes. As they pop, shake the pot a few times. When you don't hear any more popping, the popcorn is done, anywhere from 7 to 10 minutes.

In the meantime, add the butter to a small saucepan. Cook over low heat until it has melted.

Drizzle the butter over the popcorn and sprinkle with the nutritional yeast and salt. Toss around to coat all of the popcorn as evenly as you can. Top it off with more nutritional yeast, if desired.

Q & A:

WHAT'S THE STORY WITH MELTED REFINED COCONUT OIL?

Refined coconut oil is neutral in flavor and aroma, as opposed to unrefined coconut oil, which smells and tastes like coconut. Refined coconut oil is the way to go when you don't want any coconut flavor in your recipe. And because of the makeup of the fatty acids in coconut oil, it's solid and bright white at room temperature, about 68°F (20°C). When the temperature hits about 78°F (26°C), the coconut oil melts and becomes crystal clear. Measure the amount you need for a recipe after it has melted because the conversion from solid to liquid is not always exact. If your coconut oil is solid when you are ready to use it, just set it in some warm water or near a source of warm air. The change from solid to liquid (and back again) will not affect the oil in any way.

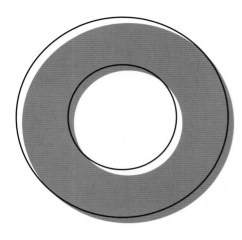

OATS

I bet you have a canister or bag of old-fashioned oats in your pantry right now. Am I right? Sometimes you make oatmeal or overnight oats, but most of the time they just sit there waiting for a good recipe to come along. Well, get ready to use up that stash and to start adding it to your regular rotation.

Oats are one of the healthiest foods on the planet. They are a naturally gluten-free whole grain that is high in fiber, protein, carbs, vitamins and minerals. But, more specifically, oats are one of the only sources of a soluble fiber called beta-glucan, which has been shown to lower cholesterol and reduce blood sugar levels.

Oats are one of the only sources of a unique group of antioxidants called avenanthramides, which have been shown to reduce blood pressure and inflammation. Considering that heart disease is one of the leading causes of death in the United States, eating oats can be lifesaving.

But don't settle for that plain, boring bowl of oatmeal. Make The Only Granola Recipe You'll Ever Need (page 109), a combination of oats, shredded coconut, nuts and dried fruit. Try it on top of a bowl of yogurt or layered in Chia-Hemp-Coconut Pudding Parfaits with Date Syrup (page 133).

Upgrade and healthify your desserts with oats. Try the Three-Berry Crumble (page 110), which is way easier than pie, or these Delicious Date-Oat Squares (page 46), which are technically dessert but healthy enough to eat for breakfast.

Whatever you do, try to eat oats a few times a week, if not every day. Your body will thank you.

THE ONLY GRANOLA RECIPE YOU'LL EVER NEED

Makes approximately
5 cups (826 g)

There is absolutely no reason to buy granola at the market when you can make your own at home. It's just nuts, seeds, dried fruit and a sweet sticky sauce. You can do it! Not only is it easy, but this recipe is totally customizable. Use any combination of any nuts you like, such as almonds, Brazil nuts, cashews, hazelnuts and macadamias, and any combination of dried fruits you like, such as dried blueberries, dried apricots and dried cherries. And, if you want extra flavor, spice it up with a few shakes of cinnamon, cardamom, allspice and/or a few scrapes of a nutmeg.

I categorize granola as breakfast, but truth be told, it can be eaten any time of day. Douse it with plant-based milk, sprinkle it on top of yogurt or send it to work or school for a nutritious on-the-go snack. Or do what I do and package it up and give it out as gifts.

Preheat the oven to 325°F (163°C). Line a half sheet pan with parchment paper.

Add the oats, shredded coconut, pine nuts, pistachio meats, walnuts, pecans, sunflower seeds, pumpkin seeds and salt to a big mixing bowl. Mix together.

To make the sticky sauce, add the maple syrup, coconut sugar, coconut oil and vanilla to a small mixing bowl and whisk together.

Pour the sauce into the oat-nut-seed mixture and mix until everything is coated with sauce.

Turn out onto the sheet pan and spread out into one even layer. Bake for 30 to 35 minutes, until golden brown. Remove from the oven and let cool on the sheet pan.

Sprinkle the dried fruit over the cooled granola and mix together.

DRY INGREDIENTS

3 cups (270 g) old-fashioned rolled oats

¼ cup (23 g) unsweetened shredded coconut

¼ cup (34 g) pine nuts

¼ cup (25 g) shelled pistachios

¼ cup (29 g) coarsely chopped walnuts

¼ cup (27 g) coarsely chopped pecans

2 tbsp (16 g) toasted unsalted sunflower seeds

2 tbsp (18 g) toasted unsalted pumpkin seeds

Pinch of salt

STICKY SAUCE

¼ cup (60 ml) maple syrup

¼ cup (48 g) coconut sugar

¼ cup (60 ml) melted refined coconut oil

2 tsp (10 ml) vanilla extract

DRIED FRUIT

⅓ cup (48 g) golden raisins

⅓ cup (48 g) Thompson raisins

⅓ cup (40 g) dried cranberries

BERRIES

1½ cups (216 g) blackberries

1½ cups (249 g) strawberries, hulled and cut into quarters

1 cup (148 g) blueberries

¼ cup (48 g) coconut sugar

1 tsp all-purpose flour

1 tsp lemon zest

1 tbsp (15 ml) fresh lemon juice

CRUMBLE

¾ cup (68 g) old-fashioned rolled oats

¼ cup (31 g) all-purpose flour

¼ cup (48 g) coconut sugar

¼ cup (57 g) vegan butter, softened

Pinch of salt

THREE-BERRY CRUMBLE

A crumble is like a no-nonsense pie. It's just the right blend of rustic and impressive. Blackberries, strawberries and blueberries are topped with a mixture of oats, flour, sugar and butter and baked until they are soft and juicy. But that topping is the real star of this show—yummy, buttery and crumbly.

Want to change it up? Go with a single berry or your favorite two-berry combos. If it's summer, you could go with stone fruits like peaches or plums. If it's winter, peel some apples or pears. The possibilities are endless!

Preheat the oven to 350°F (177°C). Place a 1-quart (946-g) baking dish on a half sheet pan.

To prepare the berries, add the blackberries, strawberries, blueberries, coconut sugar, flour, lemon zest and lemon juice to a big mixing bowl. Mix together and set aside.

To prepare the crumble, add the oats, flour, coconut sugar, butter and salt to a small mixing bowl. Use your fingers to mix everything together.

Turn out the berries into the baking dish along with any excess berry juice. Sprinkle the crumble mixture over the top of the berries.

Bake for 30 minutes. Serve warm or at room temperature.

PORTOBELLOS

Mushrooms are one of the greatest and most versatile vegan ingredients out there. They are so cool that they exist in a kingdom all of their own!

There are thousands of different kinds of mushrooms, but we generally eat the cultivated mushrooms of the Agaricus bisporus family. These include those ubiquitous little white button mushrooms, the medium-sized brown mushrooms called baby bellas or creminis and those big, gigantic portobellos.

The difference between the three is really just how old they are. The youngest is the white mushroom, which is cultivated to be white, smooth and very mild in flavor. Creminis are a little older, brown in color, firmer, more flavorful and work well in recipes that call for little mushrooms, including a bunch of recipes in this book.

The oldest, and the most mature, is the portobello mushroom. They are native to Italy and have been around since ancient times, but there was not that much interest in them abroad until the 1980s. To increase sales, they decided to give them a fancy Italian name and, boom, their popularity soared!

Portobellos are gigantic. They have flat, broad caps—that can be anywhere from 4 and 6 inches (10 and 15 cm) wide—thick, dark gills and stubby, white stems. Basically, they are overgrown white mushrooms, but much drier, with a dense, chewy and meaty texture. They have an earthy, sort of smoky flavor and are very rich in umami—the steak of the plant world! When you are out shopping for portobellos, look for ones with firm, smooth (not wrinkled) caps and dry (not slimy) gills.

Portobellos are super healthy. They are a good source of vitamins B, C and D. They are high in iron and copper and even have more potassium than a banana! They are loaded with antioxidants and have been shown to be protective against cancer and heart disease, to reduce blood pressure, moderate blood sugar and boost the immune system. They are low in fat, high in fiber and have zero cholesterol.

Portobellos are conveniently bun-sized, which makes them a simple burger swap. Season them with your favorite grill seasoning, roast or grill them whole, top them with burger toppings and enjoy an easy vegan burger. Turn them into giant stuffed mushrooms, try them in Modern Portobello Stroganoff (page 115), a plant-based take on the classic dish, or top them with pizzaiola sauce in Porto-bello Steak Pizzaiola (page 116).

Portobellos are pretty uncomplicated. They fall into the plants-in-center-of-the-plate category, like beets, eggplant, garbanzo beans, jackfruit, lentils, tofu, tempeh and zucchini. They can be sautéed, grilled or roasted and flavored up any way you want. Just have fun with the fungus!

MODERN PORTOBELLO STROGANOFF

Stroganoff is a classic dish that was created by a French chef in St. Petersburg, Russia, in 1891 for a cooking contest. He won and the rest is history! The flavors are classically French (mustard) and Russian (meat in cream) at the same time. It's really easy to veganize and modernize, with meaty portobellos and yogurt, so if you have food nostalgia like me, you are going to love it. It's just as memorable and luxurious as the original.

While it's traditional to serve stroganoff over a bed of curly noodles, it's also delicious with rice, vegan mashed potatoes and crispy roasted potatoes.

Heat a cast-iron or nonstick skillet over medium-low heat. Add the oil and butter and melt them together. Add the mushrooms, onions, garlic and paprika. Cook, mixing around occasionally, until the mushrooms have released their moisture and have significantly reduced in size and the onions are soft, about 10 minutes. Season with tamari and nutritional yeast.

Deglaze the pan with the white wine and cook until the wine is mostly absorbed, about 2 minutes. Add the yogurt and mustard and mix until the sauce is uniformly creamy.

In the meantime, prepare the noodles. Bring a big pot of salted water to a boil and cook the noodles according to the package instructions. Drain the noodles and put them back into the pot. Stir in the Chive-Parsley-Lemon Butter.

Serve the noodles topped with stroganoff and a sprinkle of parsley and chives.

STROGANOFF

2 tbsp (30 ml) good olive oil

2 tbsp (28 g) vegan butter

4 portobello mushrooms, stems and gills removed and chopped into big chunks

1 small onion, thinly sliced into quarter moons

2 cloves garlic, pressed

2 tsp (5 g) paprika

1 tbsp (15 ml) tamari

1 tbsp (5 g) nutritional yeast

½ cup (120 ml) vegan white wine

½ cup (120 ml) plain unsweetened vegan yogurt

2 tsp (10 ml) grainy mustard

NOODLES

½ lb (227 g) curly noodles

1 tbsp (14 g) Chive-Parsley-Lemon Butter (page 59)

TO SERVE

Fresh parsley, chopped

Fresh chives, chopped

PORTOBELLO STEAK PIZZAIOLA

Pizzaiola is a traditional Neapolitan dish that features meat smothered in a pizza-style sauce. There is no need for steak when you've got portobellos! But before being smothered with sauce, the portobellos are marinated with balsamic vinegar and roasted until tender and juicy for an extra flavor punch. Trust me, tomatoes and balsamic vinegar are a match made in culinary heaven! Serve with crusty bread to sop up all the extra sauce. Speaking of the sauce, make it ahead of time and store it in an airtight container in the refrigerator for up to 1 week or in the freezer for up to 6 months.

PIZZAIOLA SAUCE

1 tbsp (15 ml) good olive oil

1 small onion, diced

2 cloves garlic, pressed

1 tsp dried oregano

¼ tsp crushed red pepper

Pinch of salt

¼ cup (60 ml) vegan white wine

1 tbsp (16 g) tomato paste

1 (18.3-oz [519-g]) jar whole peeled tomatoes

PORTOBELLO STEAKS

4 portobello mushrooms, stems and gills removed

2 tbsp (30 ml) good olive oil, plus more for brushing

2 tbsp (30 ml) balsamic vinegar

Pinch of salt

Dash of pepper

TO SERVE

Seedy Sprinkle Cheese (page 79)

Fresh basil, cut in chiffonade

To prepare the sauce, heat a cast-iron or nonstick skillet over medium heat. Add the olive oil. When it's shimmering, add the onions and cook until translucent, about 5 minutes. Add the garlic, oregano, crushed red pepper and salt, and cook until the garlic is fragrant, about 1 minute. Deglaze the pan with the white wine and cook until the wine is mostly absorbed, about 2 minutes.

Add the tomato paste. Use a wooden spoon to mix the tomato paste into the onion mixture, cooking it for 3 to 4 minutes.

Add the tomatoes and gently break them up with the wooden spoon, leaving the sauce as chunky as you like. Reduce the heat to low, cover and stew the tomatoes for 20 minutes, stirring occasionally and breaking up the tomatoes more, if desired.

In the meantime, prepare the portobello steaks. Preheat the oven to 400°F (204°C). Line a half sheet pan with parchment paper.

Brush the mushroom caps with olive oil. Place them cap side down, inside side up, on the sheet pan. Whisk together the oil and balsamic vinegar and season with salt and pepper. Fill each one evenly with the oil-vinegar mixture.

Bake the mushrooms for 15 minutes, until tender and the juices are flowing. Remove from the oven and let them rest for a few minutes. Slice into thick pieces.

Served topped with pizzaiola sauce, Seedy Sprinkle Cheese and basil.

QUINOA

Quinoa has exploded in popularity over the last decade or so, but it's actually an ancient grain. It originated in the area surrounding Lake Titicaca in Peru and Bolivia more than 5,000 years ago and was a staple food of the native South American cultures.

Quinoa was considered a sacred crop, a gift from the gods. The Incas called it "the mother of all grains," and legend has it that the Incan emperor himself planted the first quinoa seeds of the season with a golden planting stick.

Quinoa was almost lost to the world. When Spanish explorers arrived in South America in the 1500s, they killed the emperor, forbade quinoa religious ceremonies, destroyed all of the quinoa fields and outlawed its cultivation. But, high up in the mountains on the Andean plateau, quinoa continued to grow wildly. The natives hid it from the conquistadors and continued to cultivate it and eat it for centuries.

In 1983, the Quinoa Corporation first imported quinoa to the United States. It was immediately embraced by health food nuts and the alternative food scene around the world. Eventually, quinoa hit the mainstream and, in 2013, the United Nations declared it the International Year of Quinoa.

Even though quinoa is classified as a grain, it's actually the seed of the flowering quinoa plant. It's botanically related to spinach and beets and one of the healthiest and most nutritious foods on the face of the earth. It's a complete protein, meaning that it contains all nine essential amino acids and making it an excellent plant-based protein source. It's also high in fiber, antioxidants, iron, magnesium and B vitamins.

Quinoa comes in different colors—white, red and black—with subtle differences in both taste and texture. White quinoa is the largest seed of the three and cooks up really fluffy and light. It has a creamy texture with a delicate natural flavor. Red quinoa seeds are medium-sized and are a pretty clay color. Red quinoa is a little heartier than white, with a slightly nutty flavor and a firm texture.

Black quinoa is the smallest seed and, when cooked, it's crunchier than both white and red, and it tastes earthy and sweet, in a vegetable kind of way. Try all three to see which color you like best. They even sell bags of all three mixed together—tricolor or rainbow quinoa—which adds different flavors, colors and textures to your recipes.

Make a batch of quinoa at the beginning of the week to have on hand to add to salads, soups and stews. Not only does it add protein, but it adds flavor and texture too. And it's easy! Just measure out what you plan to use, add it to a fine-mesh sieve and rinse it with cold water. Place it in a pot and cover it with twice the amount of water as there is quinoa. Bring it to a boil, reduce it to a simmer, cover and cook until the water is absorbed, the quinoa is all puffed up and the little curlicue tails have separated from the seeds. This can take anywhere from 10 to 15 minutes. Generally, 1 cup (170 g) of uncooked quinoa yields around 3 cups (555 g) of cooked quinoa. Cooked quinoa can be stored in an airtight container in the refrigerator for up to 1 week and in the freezer for up to 6 months.

Try it in The Big Kale Salad with Seedy Sprinkle Cheese (page 79), use it as a vehicle for vegetables in Zesty Quinoa Pilaf (page 122) or treat everyone to quinoa at breakfast and make Banana-Quinoa Buttermilk Pancakes (page 121) for a surprisingly fluffy and extra-nutritious meal!

BANANA-QUINOA BUTTERMILK PANCAKES

These pancakes are made possible with homemade buttermilk and quinoa. Seriously, is there nothing our star ingredients can't do?! Apple cider vinegar acidulates soy milk to create a quick version of cultured dairy milk, which tenderizes the gluten in the flour. Quinoa adds extra fluffiness and a slightly nutty flavor, so you end up with yummy light and airy pancakes.

To make the buttermilk, whisk together the soy milk and apple cider vinegar. Let stand for 5 minutes to acidulate. It will be lumpy.

To make the pancake batter, add the flour, coconut sugar, baking powder, cinnamon and ground nutmeg to a medium mixing bowl. Whisk together. Pour the buttermilk into the flour mixture. Whisk until the batter is smooth and there are no lumps. Let the batter stand for 5 minutes; it will puff up a bit. Add the quinoa, vanilla and salt, and mix well.

Heat a cast-iron griddle or nonstick pan and add a dollop of butter. As it sizzles, use a spatula to coat the entire pan. Scoop the batter onto the pan, being sure not to crowd it, and top each pancake with a few banana slices.

Cook until the tops start to bubble and look a little dry, about 5 minutes. Flip the pancakes over and cook for another minute. Cook for another 1 or 2 minutes, until the bananas are just caramelized. Remove the pancakes to a plate and set aside. Continue to make pancakes until all of the batter is gone, wiping the pan and adding new butter in between.

Serve with a drizzle of maple syrup and a dash of cinnamon.

BUTTERMILK
1 cup (240 ml) plain unsweetened soy milk

1 tbsp (15 ml) apple cider vinegar

PANCAKES
1 cup (125 g) all-purpose flour

2 tbsp (24 g) coconut sugar

1 tbsp (14 g) baking powder

Cinnamon, a few shakes

Nutmeg, 5 scrapes on a microplane

¼ cup (46 g) packed cooked white quinoa

1 tsp vanilla extract

Pinch of salt

Vegan butter, for cooking

1 banana, sliced into thin rounds

TO SERVE
Maple syrup

Cinnamon

Serves 4 to 6

1 tbsp (15 ml) good olive oil

1 leek, white and light green parts, cleaned and cut into half-moons

1 carrot, cut into thin rounds

1 clove garlic, pressed

1 medium-sized zucchini, cut into wedges

12 asparagus spears, woody ends trimmed and cut into thin rounds

Pinch of salt

Dash of pepper

3 cups (555 g) cooked quinoa

½ cup (67 g) toasted unsalted sunflower seeds

TO SERVE

Fresh parsley, chopped

Lemon zest

ZESTY QUINOA PILAF

The first time I ever had quinoa was at a little organic specialty food shop in a small town I used to live in. The owner, who became a mentor and friend, gave me this recipe, a delicious and colorful combination of quinoa, leeks, carrots, zucchini and asparagus. And it's not just about the vegetables. Nutty, buttery sunflower seeds and lots of lemon zest top it all off to make this a light, healthy and pretty way to showcase quinoa.

Heat a pan with sides over medium heat. Add the olive oil. When it's shimmering, add the leeks and carrots and cook until the leeks become translucent and the carrots start to soften, about 10 minutes. Add the garlic, zucchini, asparagus, salt and pepper, and cook for another 5 minutes, until the zucchini and asparagus are tender and bright green.

Add the quinoa and sunflower seeds to a big mixing bowl. Add the vegetables and mix together well.

Top with parsley and lemon zest and serve warm or at room temperature.

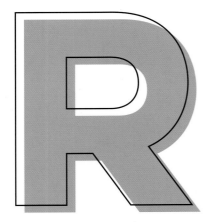

RICE

It is believed that rice has fed more humans over more millennia than any other crop. It was domesticated from wild grass in the region of the Yangtze River valley in China more than 10,000 years ago. From there, its cultivation spread from India to the Mediterranean to Southern Europe to Northern Africa and eventually to the Americas.

Rice is an extremely versatile crop and can grow almost anywhere. In fact, today it's grown in over 100 countries and on every continent, except Antarctica! It has played a role in the development of cultures and societies all over the world, inspiring everything from myths, legends and religious beliefs to songs, paintings and festivals.

Rice is thrown over a bride and groom, a very old custom that predates Christianity, variously representing luck, growth, health, fertility, good fortune and prosperity. And no, rice is not bad for the birds. That's an urban myth.

Rice is often the first solid food fed to babies in the form of cereal because it's easy to digest and full of nutrients—albeit kind of bland and boring! And there is even a rice theory that says that growing rice fosters a culture of cooperation, coordination and collaboration. I love that!

Rice is an incredibly diverse ingredient and is a part of almost every cuisine on the planet. Think about it. Spanish dishes like arroz con pollo and paella. Italian dishes like arancini and risotto. Indian dishes like biryani and khichdi. Chinese dishes like sizzling rice and congee. Japanese dishes like sushi and onigiri. American dishes like jambalaya and dirty rice. It can also be made into drinks like horchata and sake, desserts like mochi and rice pudding, and milled into flour, noodles and cereal.

There are thousands of varieties of rice, but generally speaking, there are three basic groups—short, medium and long grain—based on their length-to-width ratio. Long-grain rice is four to five times as long as it is wide, medium grain is about two to three times and short grain is round and fat and wider than it is long.

Long-grain rice includes varieties like basmati, texmati and jasmine. They are aromatic but mild in flavor and the grains stay fluffy and distinct when cooked. Long grains are the best choice for dishes like pilafs and Vegetable Jambalaya (page 128).

Short-grain rice is sticky and starchy and clumps up when it's cooked. Short-grain varieties include bomba, which is used in paella; sweet rice, which is used in rice pudding; and sushi rice, which is used in, you guessed it, sushi!

Medium-grain rice is right in the middle, not as distinct as long grain but also not as starchy as short grain. It's fluffy right after it's cooked but clumps up as it cools. Medium-grain varieties include arborio, carnaroli and vialone nano, which is the kind of rice used to make Risotto with Peas and Fresh Herbs (page 127).

The moral of the story is that the length of the grain determines the texture of the cooked rice, which is important depending on the dish you are making. And since rice is a staple ingredient around the world, it's good to know which rice is best to use for which dish.

Rice can be an exciting and tasty ingredient in plant-based cooking. Just be sure to add interesting textures and season it up with lots of herbs and spices! Serve it alongside a saucy main dish or create dishes with rice as the main ingredient like XO Fried Rice (page 171).

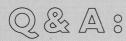

WHAT IS THE BEST WAY TO COOK PLAIN RICE?

There are a lot of conflicting opinions. Some people rinse rice before cooking. Some people bring the rice and water to a boil together with an exact 2:1 ratio of water to rice, while others boil the water first and cook rice like pasta. Some people cook it with the lid on and others with the lid off. Some people add vegan butter and salt. Some people use a rice cooker. So, what is the answer? There is no answer! I have tried all different ways and I honestly can't tell you that one way is better than another. Cook it how you want to, but just be sure it tastes good!

RISOTTO WITH PEAS AND FRESH HERBS

Risotto is a classic Northern Italian rice dish that is made with special medium-grain, high-starch rice varieties like arborio, carnaroli and vialone nano. Making risotto is actually more of a technique than a dish and should take no more than half an hour from start to finish. First, sauté some aromatics. Then slowly add warm liquid a little at a time until it's fully absorbed. The slow cooking process coaxes out the starches in the rice and, with the addition of a little vegan butter, the result is creamy and delicious.

Risotto is totally customizable. Go with water to keep it light or use vegetable broth for an extra layer of flavor. Use any vegetables and herbs you love!

4 cups (960 ml) water or vegetable broth

1 tbsp (15 ml) good olive oil

4 shallots, thinly sliced

2 cloves garlic, pressed

Pinch of salt

1 cup (200 g) uncooked arborio, carnaroli, vialone nano or other medium-grain rice

1 cup (240 ml) vegan white wine

1 sprig fresh thyme

1 cup (134 g) frozen peas

1 tbsp (14 g) Shallot-Thyme Butter (page 59)

TO SERVE

Fresh parsley, chopped

Lemon zest

Bring the water or vegetable broth to a boil. Turn the heat to low to keep it warm.

Heat a wide shallow pan over medium-low heat. Add the olive oil. When it's shimmering, add the shallots, garlic and salt. Cook until the shallots become translucent and start to soften, about 8 minutes. Add the rice and toss around to coat with oil. Cook for about 2 minutes, until the grains start to look translucent. Add the white wine, stir occasionally and cook until the wine is absorbed. Add the sprig of thyme.

Add a ladle or two of water or broth to the rice. Cook, stirring occasionally with a wooden spoon, until the liquid is almost completely absorbed. To determine when to add the next ladle of liquid, run the wooden spoon across the bottom of the pan. It should leave a dry path. Continue to add ladles of liquid, stirring occasionally and cooking until it is absorbed.

Start tasting the risotto at the 15-minute mark to gauge how far it has already cooked. You will know it's done when the rice is creamy, al dente and the consistency of a thick porridge. When you run the wooden spoon through the risotto, it should slowly flow back into the empty space.

To finish the risotto, add the peas and Shallot-Thyme Butter and stir into the risotto. Cover and let stand for 2 minutes.

Remove the sprig of thyme and serve topped with parsley and lemon zest.

Serves 4

1 tbsp (15 ml) sunflower oil

1 red onion, cut into thick strips

½ green bell pepper, cut into strips

½ yellow bell pepper, cut into strips

1 rib celery, cut into chunks

1 carrot, cut into rounds

8 oz (227 g) baby bella mushrooms, cut into quarters

2 cloves garlic, pressed

1 tsp crushed red pepper

1 tsp Old Bay seasoning

1 tsp dried oregano

½ tsp cumin

Cayenne pepper, a few shakes, optional

Pinch of salt

2 tbsp (32 g) tomato paste

2 tbsp (10 g) nutritional yeast

1 tbsp (15 ml) tamari

1 cup (200 g) uncooked long-grain white rice

3 cups (720 ml) vegetable broth

3 sprigs fresh thyme

1 bay leaf

1 tsp sherry vinegar

TO SERVE
Fresh parsley, chopped

VEGETABLE JAMBALAYA

Jambalaya is a big, flavorful, one-pot, crowd-pleasing rice-based dish that is thought to have originated in the French Quarter in New Orleans. The story goes that that they wanted to make paella, another rice dish, but there was no saffron, the main flavor ingredient of the dish. So instead, they subbed tomatoes and seasoned it with local flavors. I use lots of Old Bay, oregano and fresh thyme to invoke those flavors and pack it with meaty mushrooms and lots of bell peppers. If you like it spicy, add a few shakes of cayenne pepper. No matter what you do, serve it topped with fresh parsley for a bit of freshness and color.

Heat a heavy-bottomed pot over medium heat. Add the sunflower oil. When it's shimmering, add the onions, bell peppers, celery, carrots and mushrooms. Cook until the vegetables just start to soften, about 5 minutes. Add the garlic, crushed red pepper, Old Bay, oregano, cumin, cayenne pepper (if using) and salt. Mix around and cook until the garlic is fragrant, about 1 minute.

Add the tomato paste. Use a wooden spoon to mix it into the vegetables, cooking it for 3 to 4 minutes. Add the nutritional yeast and tamari, and stir it into the vegetables.

Add the rice and toss to mix it in thoroughly. Add the vegetable broth, thyme and bay leaf. Bring to a boil, reduce to a simmer, cover and cook until the broth is absorbed, 15 to 20 minutes, until the rice is al dente.

Take it off the heat and stir in the sherry vinegar. Remove the thyme sprigs and bay leaf. Cover and let stand for 5 minutes.

When ready to serve, fluff up the jambalaya and top with parsley.

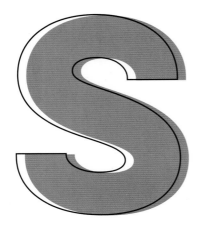

SEEDS

Seeds are small but mighty ingredients. Each one has its own unique flavor, texture, nutrition profile and health benefits, and each can be used in a variety of ways, separately and together. Always be on the lookout for ways to add seeds to your meals.

Chia seeds are from a flowering plant in the mint family native to Mexico and Guatemala. They were highly prized and considered magical by the ancient Aztecs and Mayans because of the amount of energy and stamina they provided to the warriors and running messengers. Today, they are a super-popular super-food for those very same reasons. Here's why.

Chia seeds are the richest plant-based source of omega-3s and super high in protein and dietary fiber. They are abundant in vitamins A, B, D, E and K and minerals like calcium, iron, magnesium, potassium and zinc. Not only that, chia seeds regulate carbohydrate conversion, prevent blood sugar spikes, provide sustained energy and regulate hydration. Chia seeds have a neutral flavor and, unlike flaxseed, are digestible whether consumed ground up (like over a salad or in a smoothie) or whole. But whole chia seeds are the coolest! They absorb about ten times their weight in liquid and puff up into little gel bubbles. You will see how they work in these Chia-Hemp-Coconut Pudding Parfaits with Date Syrup (page 133).

Hemp seeds won't get you high, even though they are from the same plant as pot, because they only contain trace amounts of THC, but you should eat them anyway. Hemp seeds are a complete protein, meaning that they contain all nine essential amino acids, and are rich in healthy fats, omega-6s, omega-3s and vitamin E. They are good for the skin, aid digestion and have even been shown to reduce symptoms associated with perimenopause.

Add hemp seeds to salads like The Big Kale Salad with Seedy Sprinkle Cheese (page 79) and Balsamic Tempeh Dragon Bowls (page 139).

Sesame seeds are a good source of healthy fats, protein, B vitamins, minerals, fiber and antioxidants. They are crunchy, nutty and buttery and, for such little guys, they add a surprising amount of flavor and texture to all kinds of dishes. They are especially complementary to the flavors of Asian-inspired recipes like Miso Eggplant (page 37) and Cold Sesame Noodles (page 145).

When you are out shopping for sesame seeds, grab a little jar of toasted sesame seeds to use in recipes that call for them as a garnish and a bag of hulled sesame seeds to use for recipes like Super Seed Bars (page 134).

Sesame seed paste, better known as tahini, is made from ground toasted sesame seeds. It's like the sophisticated cousin of peanut and almond butter. Tahini is nutty and rich, but also slightly bitter and kind of mysterious. You will fully under- stand when you make lemony garlicky Tahini Dressing (page 52), which you just might want to put on everything or when you taste Tofu Ricotta (page 140).

Pumpkin seeds, a.k.a. pepitas, are oval, flat, green, shelled seeds that are jam-packed with nutrients and antioxidants, including iron, zinc, magnesium, fiber, phosphorus and omega-6s. They have been shown to improve heart health, blood sugar levels, energy, mood, immune function, fertility and sleep quality and may even protect against certain types of cancer.

Pumpkin seeds are delicious simply roasted, salted and sprinkled over salads. They add texture and flavor to The Only Granola Recipe You'll Ever Need (page 109) and add crunch to Shredded Beet Tacos with Tomatillo Salsa (page 19) and Jackfruit Tacos al Pastor with Pineapple Salsa (page 74).

Sunflower seeds are actually the fruit of those big yellow sunflowers. You know those gorgeous dark centers? They hold something like 2,000 edible seeds that form a spiral pattern that follows the Fibonacci sequence. So, not just nutrition, but math too!

Sunflower seeds are high in vitamin E and antioxidants and have been shown to reduce inflammation. They are mild and nutty in a sunflowery kind of way. Look for shelled sunflower seeds and add them for flavor and texture to Zesty Quinoa Pilaf (page 122), The Only Granola Recipe You'll Ever Need (page 109) and Seedy Sprinkle Cheese (page 79).

One more thing: Since both pumpkin seeds and sunflower seeds can be eaten raw or toasted, I like to buy them raw and toast them at home. It's easy! Preheat the oven to 325°F (163°C), line a half sheet pan with parchment paper and arrange the seeds in a single layer. Bake for 10 to 15 minutes, until the seeds are fragrant and have turned a shade darker. Remove the pan from the oven, let them cool and then store them in an airtight container in the refrigerator to use anytime you want!

CHIA-HEMP-COCONUT PUDDING PARFAITS WITH DATE SYRUP

Makes 2

Remember how chia seeds puff up into little gel bubbles when they are hydrated? Well, soaking them in coconut milk results in a dessert that is similar in texture to tapioca pudding but tastes sweet, floral and nutty. By itself, the pudding is a treat, but when it's layered with crunchy granola and bananas, it's even better. And then, to top it all off? That biblical honey—date syrup. It's dark, rich, luscious, sweet and utterly divine. You are going to want to put it on everything, not just these parfaits!

To make the date syrup, add the dates to a big bowl, cover with water and soak for 1 hour. Use a potato masher to mash them up a bit.

Add the mashed dates and soaking water to a pot. Bring to a boil, reduce to a simmer and cook, until the dates have completely broken down and have turned a sort of dark, almost purple color, about 30 minutes. Cool completely.

Set up a nut milk bag over a bowl. Add the cooked dates and squeeze as much of the liquid out as possible. Discard the pulpy remains.

Pour the liquid into a small saucepan and set it over low heat. Cook it down until it's reduced to a thick dark syrup, stirring occasionally, about 20 to 25 minutes. Turn off the heat, cover and let cool. Store in an airtight container in the refrigerator and use within 2 weeks.

To make the pudding, add the coconut milk, chia seeds, hemp seeds, maple syrup, shredded coconut, ground vanilla and salt to a pint-sized (473-ml) lidded jar. Cover and shake well, in order to avoid clumps of chia seeds. Refrigerate for at least 4 hours or overnight.

Evenly divide the pudding into 2 cups or bowls. Serve layered with granola, bananas and date syrup.

DATE SYRUP

1 lb (454 g) pitted Medjool dates

4 cups (960 ml) water

CHIA-HEMP-COCONUT PUDDING

1 cup (240 ml) reduced-fat unsweetened coconut milk

3 tbsp (30 g) chia seeds

2 tbsp (20 g) hemp seeds

1 tbsp (15 ml) maple syrup

1 tsp unsweetened shredded coconut

¼ tsp ground vanilla

Pinch of salt

PARFAITS

The Only Granola Recipe You'll Ever Need (page 109)

Bananas, sliced into thin rounds

Makes 10

SUPER SEED BARS

These bars are packed with all six seeds highlighted in this book—pumpkin, sunflower, sesame, hemp, chia and flaxseed—which means they are protein-packed nutritional powerhouses. Eat them anytime you need a pick-me-up, take them on your next hike or scarf them down after a workout.

SEEDS

¾ cup (104 g) toasted unsalted pumpkin seeds

¾ cup (101 g) toasted unsalted sunflower seeds

¼ cup (36 g) hulled sesame seeds

¼ cup (40 g) hemp seeds

2 tbsp (20 g) chia seeds

1 tbsp (10 g) ground flaxseed

STICKY SAUCE

½ cup (120 ml) maple syrup

2 tbsp (28 g) vegan butter

1 tbsp (15 ml) tahini

1 tsp vanilla extract

Add the pumpkin seeds, sunflower seeds, sesame seeds, hemp seeds, chia seeds and ground flaxseed to a big mixing bowl. Mix together.

To make the sticky sauce, add the maple syrup, butter, tahini and vanilla to a small saucepan. Turn the heat on low and whisk together until the butter is melted and the sauce is combined.

Pour the sauce over the seeds and mix thoroughly. Let stand for 15 minutes.

In the meantime, preheat the oven to 350°F (177°C). Line an 8 x 8-inch (20.5 x 20.5-cm) baking pan with parchment paper.

Turn out the seed mixture into the baking pan. Spread it out into an even layer, pressing the mixture to the edges of the pan.

Bake for 1 hour.

Let cool for a few minutes. Lift by the parchment paper and transfer to a cooling rack to cool completely before cutting into bars.

TEMPEH AND TOFU

When it comes to plant-based food, it doesn't get any more vegan than tempeh and tofu. They are both thousands of years old, with tofu originating in China and tempeh in Indonesia. In fact, tempeh is the only major traditional soy food that did not originate in China or Japan. Today, they are both popular ingredients all over the world and staples in a vegan kitchen.

Let's start with tofu. You might be familiar with the plain, white, square block of . . . wait, what is it exactly? It's actually curdled soy milk! Before you freak out, because that sounds weird, understand that it's made essentially the same way as dairy cheese. A coagulant is added to soy milk to curdle it. The curds are separated from the whey and pressed into blocks. Then, it's packaged up so we can buy tons of it to make all kinds of things.

On its own, tofu doesn't really taste like anything, which is fine because you are never going to eat it plain. It's precisely because it tastes like nothing that tofu can be anything. You know what I mean? Tofu can be marinated, breaded, baked, grilled, pan-fried, sautéed, cubed, crumbled and scrambled. For example, when it's seasoned with a few of our other star ingredients, it becomes a very tasty dairy-free Tofu Ricotta (page 140). When it's seasoned with Indian black salt, it's transformed into all of the delicious eggy breakfast things. And in Tofu Satay with Coconut-Peanut Sauce (page 26), it's marinated and baked, highlighting its texture and just how flavorful it can be.

Tofu is sold in varying consistencies, depending on the water content. Silken tofu contains the most water and extra firm contains the least, with soft, firm and super firm in between. The less water, the firmer the tofu. The firmer the tofu, the meatier the texture. But even then, each brand defines firmness differently, so you might have to try a few before you decide which works best for the recipe you are making.

The natural water content in the tofu affects the overall texture and outcome of a recipe, which is why some recipes call for pressing it. You can buy a tofu press, but if you are not ready to invest in one, you can make your own. Wrap the block of tofu in paper towels or a kitchen towel and place it in a bowl or on a tray. Place a heavy pot or a couple of cans on top and let it sit for at least 10 minutes or however long the recipe calls for.

Now let's talk about tempeh. Tempeh is made from cooked and fermented soybeans that are pressed into a square or rectangular cake, although it can also be made out of beans and grains. Because it's fermented, tempeh is loaded with a complex umami flavor. It's sort of nutty and earthy, but also slightly bitter with a kind of fermented tang. As for the texture, it's dense and dry and somewhat chewy. And yes, it's definitely an acquired taste.

Tempeh is not quite as well known and ubiquitous as tofu, but you should still be able to find it, if not at the regular market then at a local health food store. Most places stock it in the refrigerated aisle, but sometimes it's in the freezer case. If you happen to have a local tempeh maker in your area, like I do here in New York, definitely buy your tempeh from them.

When you open a package of tempeh, you will see that it looks like compressed beans, because that is exactly what it is. Sometimes there are black or dark gray areas on the surface of the tempeh, which is the result of the cultures used to ferment the beans. It's totally fine; you don't have to cut it away.

Tempeh should always be cooked and can be sautéed, baked and grilled. After years of working with tempeh, I have come to the conclusion that it's best to steam it before proceeding with any recipe. It reduces the bitterness and softens it up, making it more available to absorb flavors and marinades.

From a nutritional point of view, tempeh and tofu are incredibly healthy. Tempeh is rich in prebiotics and is higher in fiber than tofu, but tofu is higher in calcium than tempeh. Both are complete proteins, meaning that they contain all nine essential amino acids, and are cholesterol free!

Both tempeh and tofu are high in iron, calcium, manganese, phosphorous, potassium, magnesium, copper, zinc, B vitamins and rich in a class of phytoestrogens called isoflavones, which have been shown to reduce the risk of developing heart disease and certain cancers.

Get to know tempeh and tofu well. The recipes in this book are only a sample of their versatility. Go through your recipe box, find your favorite marinades and sauces, use the techniques and instructions for prepping and start experimenting!

Q & A:
DOES EATING SOY CAUSE BREAST CANCER?

The short answer is no. The long answer has to do with the fact that soy foods contain isoflavones, a type of plant estrogen also called phytoestrogen, that is similar in function to human estrogen but with much weaker effects. Because high levels of estrogen have been linked to an increased risk of breast cancer, the question naturally follows; however, soy foods like tempeh and tofu don't contain high enough levels of isoflavones to increase cancer risk. In fact, human studies have found that consuming soy is actually beneficial and even protective against breast cancer. Visit www.cancer.org for more information.

BALSAMIC TEMPEH DRAGON BOWLS

Makes 4

Back in the day, I used to eat at Angelica Kitchen, one of New York City's original vegan restaurants. This recipe is an ode to their famous dragon bowls, named for the pretty bowls they were served in. But it's really just a big salad!

Tempeh is marinated in a sweet, complex, musky balsamic vinegar marinade and baked until just crispy around the edges. Then, it's piled on top of mixed greens and surrounded by sweet beets, hearty barley, Pickled Red Onions (page 152) and a seedy avocado. Change it up and add whatever whole grains and vegetables you have on hand.

Place the tempeh in a pot and cover with water. Bring to a boil, reduce to a simmer and cook, uncovered, for 10 minutes.

Preheat the oven to 400°F (204°C). Line a quarter sheet pan with parchment paper.

In a medium mixing bowl, whisk together the balsamic vinegar, maple syrup, tamari and olive oil.

When the tempeh has finished simmering, drain it and drop it into the marinade, flipping it over to coat both sides. Place the tempeh on the sheet pan and pour any extra marinade over the top of the tempeh. Bake for 25 to 30 minutes, until the tempeh is crispy around the edges.

To assemble, add the greens to the bowls. Arrange the tempeh, beets and barley over the greens and add the Pickled Red Onions over the top. Sprinkle the avocado halves with hemp seeds and place one in each bowl. Serve with dressing or vinaigrette on the side.

BALSAMIC TEMPEH

1 (8-oz [227-g]) package soy tempeh, cut into 8 triangles

1 tbsp (15 ml) balsamic vinegar

1 tbsp (15 ml) maple syrup

1 tbsp (15 ml) tamari

1 tbsp (15 ml) good olive oil

BOWL

Mixed greens

2 cups (400 g) shredded raw beets

2 cups (314 g) cooked barley

Pickled Red Onions (page 152)

HEMP SEED AVOCADO

2 avocados, pitted and cut in half

Hemp seeds

TO SERVE

Tahini Dressing (page 52) or a Vinaigrette (page 155)

Makes 16 rolls

LASAGNA ROLLS WITH TOFU RICOTTA

If tofu is made using the same process as cheese, then tofu ricotta is a no-brainer. With some vegan kitchen magic in the form of nutritional yeast, umeboshi paste and tahini, tofu is transformed into a creamy, cheesy, salty, plant-based ricotta that is reminiscent in both taste and texture to dairy ricotta. Use it anywhere you would use ricotta, like on vegan pizza, in a pasta bake, stuffed in zucchini blossoms or in these lasagna rolls.

Lasagna rolls are an easy and fun way to have your lasagna and eat it too. Since they are little individual bundles, you can make as many as you want. And, if you are saucy, heat any leftover sauce and serve it alongside your rolls!

TOFU RICOTTA

1 (14-oz [397-g]) package firm tofu, drained

2 tbsp (10 g) nutritional yeast

2 tbsp (36 g) umeboshi paste

1 tbsp (15 ml) tahini

1 clove garlic, pressed

1 tbsp (15 ml) fresh lemon juice

1 tbsp (15 ml) good olive oil

½ tsp ume plum vinegar

¼ tsp salt

Nutmeg, 10 scrapes on a microplane

FILLING

1 big zucchini, shredded

2 tbsp (5 g) chopped fresh basil

2 tbsp (8 g) chopped fresh parsley

1 tbsp (6 g) lemon zest

LASAGNA ROLLS

1 tbsp (15 ml) good olive oil, plus more for oiling

1 box uncooked lasagna noodles

Your favorite tomato sauce

To make the tofu ricotta, break up the tofu and add it to the bowl of a food processor. Add the nutritional yeast, umeboshi paste, tahini, garlic, lemon juice, olive oil, ume plum vinegar, salt and ground nutmeg. Pulse a few times, until the tofu breaks down, and then process until smooth and creamy, scraping down the sides of the bowl, as necessary.

Make the ricotta ahead of time and store it in an airtight container in the refrigerator for up to 3 days or in the freezer for up to 6 months. Bring it to room temperature before proceeding with the recipe.

To prepare the filling, add the tofu ricotta to a big mixing bowl. Add the shredded zucchini, basil, parsley and lemon zest. Use a silicone spatula to fold everything together. Mix until combined. Set aside.

To make the lasagna noodles, bring a big pot of salted water with 1 tablespoon (15 ml) of olive oil to a boil. Lightly oil a sheet pan and have it ready. Cook the lasagna noodles for 5 to 7 minutes, until they are very pliable (roll-uppable). Drain into a colander and run them under cold water, swooshing the noodles around so they don't stick together. Lift them out and lay them in a single layer on the sheet pan. It's okay if they just slightly overlap. Cover with a kitchen towel and set aside.

Preheat the oven to 350°F (177°C).

Ladle tomato sauce on the bottom of a baking dish and spread it around.

Spread the ricotta mixture along the length of each lasagna noodle, leaving a little room at one end so the rolls are easy to seal. Roll them up and place them standing up in the baking dish, placing each roll close to the next, with the seams touching, to help keep them together, until all of the rolls are done. Pour more sauce over the top.

Cover with tinfoil and bake for 25 minutes. Uncover and cook until the edges look crispy and the sauce is bubbling, about 5 to 10 minutes.

UMEBOSHI

Umeboshi, made from ume plums, is an ancient Japanese ingredient and an important part of Japanese cuisine. In the vegan kitchen, it's another ingredient that adds layers of flavor to all kinds of dishes. Bottom line? It's freaking fantastic.

Ume plums have a long history. They were brought into battle by the samurai, used to purify water and fight diseases. But they may be most famous as a modern hangover cure because they stimulate and detoxify the liver. Not only that, but umeboshi is an excellent source of iron and calcium and has powerful antioxidant qualities.

Umeboshi is the fruit of the ume tree, a relative of the apricot and the plum, that has been salted, fermented, dried, pickled and aged. At some point during the process, red shiso leaves are added to the brine, resulting in a pretty ruby-color liquid, which is bottled up and called ume plum vinegar. The whole thing takes weeks, if not months, and sometimes even years. I read somewhere that the oldest umeboshi found in Japan is estimated to have been pickled in 1576 and is still edible today!

To make umeboshi paste, ume plums are simply pureed. When you are out shopping for umeboshi paste, be sure to read the label. There should only be three ingredients—ume plums, shiso leaves and salt. That's it. Nothing artificial, no preservatives. Put it back if it has artificial red dye and try another market or go home and order it online. If you happen to find ume plums, make your own paste by pitting them and dropping them into your food processor.

What does umeboshi taste like? It's the best combination of fruity, sweet, salty, briny, sour, tart and tangy. In other words: umami. You only need to use a tablespoon or two to get the full effect. Make some rice and top it with a dollop of umeboshi paste. Slather it on corn on the cob instead of butter. Or lick it off of a spoon. You just have to try it once to know it's true.

Make ume-centric recipes like Umeboshi-Roasted Cauliflower and Broccoli (page 146) and Cold Sesame Noodles (page 145). If you have a recipe for pasta puttanesca, sub umeboshi for the anchovies or add it to pesto in place of Parmesan. It makes the most delicious dressing for Zucchini Carpaccio with Fresh Herbs and Umeboshi Vinaigrette (page 181) and transforms plain tofu into tasty Tofu Ricotta (page 140).

Now that you know, get creative and start experimenting. Once you get started using umeboshi, you won't be able to stop!

COLD SESAME NOODLES

These noodles are inspired by Chef Shorty Tang, who came to New York City from the Taiwan Province of China and opened a Sichuan restaurant called Hwa Yuan in Chinatown in 1971. The place was famous for Chef Tang's signature dish, Cold Noodles with Sesame Sauce. They are legendary at this point and the recipe is still a family secret. But that hasn't stopped everyone from trying to re-create it, including me.

I've worked out a sweet-salty-spicy peanut-butter-tahini-based sauce using umeboshi, tamari, maple syrup, apple cider vinegar, garlic, ginger and crushed red pepper. If just reading that sentence doesn't make you want to run into the kitchen, I don't know what will! And wait until you taste it tossed with earthy, nutty soba noodles. Oh. My. Goodness. It's totally out of this world. And guess what? It's yet another sauce that can be made ahead of time! Store it in an airtight container in the refrigerator for up to 1 week or in the freezer for up to 6 months.

Bring a big pot of water to a boil and cook the soba noodles according to the package instructions. Drain into a colander and run the noodles under cold water, swooshing them around to wash off the starches. Set aside.

To make the sauce, add the water, umeboshi paste, tamari, peanut butter, tahini, maple syrup, apple cider vinegar, garlic, ginger and crushed red pepper to a mixing bowl. Whisk to combine.

Pour the sauce over the noodles and toss to coat well. Serve topped with the cucumbers, chives and sesame seeds.

NOODLES
½ lb (227 g) soba noodles

SAUCE
2 tbsp (30 ml) water

1 tbsp (18 g) umeboshi paste

1 tbsp (15 ml) tamari

1 tbsp (16 g) peanut butter, room temperature

1 tbsp (15 ml) tahini, room temperature

1 tbsp (15 ml) maple syrup

1 tbsp (15 ml) apple cider vinegar

1 clove garlic, pressed

1 tsp grated fresh ginger

1 tsp crushed red pepper

TO SERVE
1 Persian cucumber, thinly sliced

2 tbsp (6 g) chopped fresh chives

1 tbsp (9 g) toasted sesame seeds

Serves 4 to 6

UMEBOSHI-ROASTED CAULIFLOWER AND BROCCOLI

MARINADE

2 tbsp (36 g) umeboshi paste

2 tbsp (30 ml) sunflower oil

1 tbsp (15 ml) maple syrup

1 tbsp (15 ml) tamari

CAULIFLOWER AND BROCCOLI

1 head cauliflower, cut into florets

1 head broccoli, cut into florets

This is the marinade to end all marinades. If you know some kids who don't like cauliflower and broccoli, or if you know some picky adults who don't, the combination of umeboshi paste, maple syrup and tamari will absolutely, 100 percent change their minds. Roasting cauliflower and broccoli together makes for a great combination of textures; the broccoli comes out super crispy, while the cauliflower becomes soft and tender. Together, they work perfectly. Here's an idea: Serve with garbanzo beans, rice and a dusting of Seedy Sprinkle Cheese (page 79) for a complete meal.

Preheat the oven to 425°F (218°C). Line a half sheet pan with parchment paper.

To make the marinade, add the umeboshi paste, sunflower oil, maple syrup and tamari to a medium mixing bowl. Whisk together.

Toss the cauliflower and broccoli in the marinade, coating the florets well. Turn out onto the sheet pan.

Roast for 35 to 40 minutes, until the broccoli is charred and the cauliflower is tender.

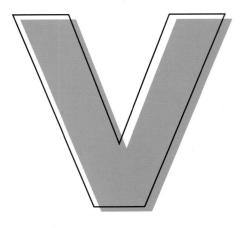

VINEGAR

Good food just cannot happen without vinegar! It's an essential pantry staple in any kitchen, like salt and pepper, and another fermented ingredient like miso, tempeh and umeboshi.

Vinegar is as old as civilization itself. It was used by the ancient Egyptians, Babylonians and Persians to preserve and pickle food and was a common drink in ancient Greece and Rome. The Romans mixed vinegar with water in a drink they called posca, which was believed to give strength. In fact, the Bible says that Roman soldiers offered posca to Jesus at the crucifixion.

Vinegar is the end product of a two-step fermentation process. Sugar is converted to alcohol and then the alcohol is converted into acetic acid. It's the acetic acid that gives vinegar its pungent smell and sour taste. The first vinegar was probably made from wine, since the word vinegar comes from the French *vin aigre*, meaning sour wine.

There are all different kinds of vinegar on the market, each with their own flavor profile and uses. I have a pantry full of them; they never go bad. Vinegar is self-preserving because of its acidic nature.

Apple cider vinegar is probably the most versatile vinegar there is. It's kind of tart, but also kind of neutral, so it works in a ton of different recipes, from mayo to cupcakes to marinades to sauces to pancakes. Buy a big bottle, because you will be using it often.

White wine vinegar is crisp, a touch fruity and light in color. I love using it to pickle vegetables because it doesn't affect the natural color of the vegetables. Red wine vinegar is a little bolder and a little sharper than white wine vinegar and makes a great vinaigrette, works well in sauces and turns pickled red onions and radishes pink.

Sherry vinegar is made from sherry wine and is my favorite vinegar for finishing sauces, soups and stews. It also makes a very sophisticated vinaigrette.

Ume plum vinegar is the pretty ruby-color pickling brine from fermented ume plums. It's not technically vinegar, but it's used the same way. It's fruity and briny and kind of magical. Buy a bottle. It's worth going to whatever trouble you have to go to to get some. But if you can't find it and have to sub it out, go with sherry vinegar.

Balsamic vinegar is a little different than the rest in that it only goes through one round of fermentation and is aged in barrels, like wine, which makes it rich in umami. Good balsamic vinegar is thick and syrupy with a rich, complex flavor and a deep, dark, beautiful color. When you buy balsamic vinegar, make sure the only ingredient is grape must, or else it's not authentic. White balsamic vinegar is a lighter version of regular balsamic, but it's golden in color, fruity and floral and just a touch sweet.

Vinegar is an extraordinarily versatile ingredient. It leavens cupcakes, acidulates buttermilk, does serious work in marinades, balances fats in sauces and makes outstanding dressing. It's the ingredient that brings out the best in every other ingredient. So when you finish making something like a soup or a stew and you taste it and it needs something—not salt, but something—reach for a bottle of vinegar. A teaspoon is usually just the thing to round out the flavors of any dish.

So, stock your pantry and try all the different vinegars. They last forever and they do it all, so why not?!

Makes approximately 1 cup (155 g) each

PICKLED RED ONIONS

1 red onion, cut into thin rings

¼ cup (60 ml) white wine vinegar

¼ cup (60 ml) red wine vinegar

¼ cup (60 ml) water

1 tbsp (15 g) sugar

Pinch of salt

PICKLED JALAPEÑOS

2 to 4 jalapeños, cut into thin rings

½ cup (120 ml) white wine vinegar

¼ cup (60 ml) water

1 tbsp (15 g) sugar

Pinch of salt

PICKLED CARROTS

2 to 3 carrots, peeled into ribbons with a vegetable peeler

1 clove garlic, cut in half

1 sprig fresh thyme

½ cup (120 ml) white wine vinegar

¼ cup (60 ml) water

1 tbsp (15 g) sugar

Pinch of salt

PICKLED CUCUMBERS

2 Persian cucumbers, cut into thin rounds

1 sprig fresh dill

1 tsp mustard seeds

½ cup (120 ml) white wine vinegar

¼ cup (60 ml) water

1 tbsp (15 g) sugar

Pinch of salt

PICKLED RADISHES

3 big or 6 small radishes, thinly sliced on a mandoline

½ tsp black peppercorns

¼ cup (60 ml) white wine vinegar

¼ cup (60 ml) red wine vinegar

¼ cup (60 ml) water

1 tbsp (15 g) sugar

Pinch of salt

PICKLED BEETS

1 to 2 small beets, peeled and thinly sliced on a mandoline

1 sprig fresh dill

½ cup (120 ml) white wine vinegar

¼ cup (60 ml) water

1 tbsp (15 g) sugar

Pinch of salt

HOW TO QUICK PICKLE ANYTHING

It's no secret. You can pickle almost any vegetable and turn them into cool, crisp, acidic pops of flavor that brighten up almost any recipe. Add them to sandwiches, salads, tacos or even sneak them for a snack all on their own.

My pickling brine formula is a ratio of 2:1 of vinegar to water, acidic but not too acidic, plus a little salt and a little sugar. Use either vegan cane sugar or coconut sugar. If you use coconut sugar, the pickling liquid will become a caramelly brown color and the vegetables will turn a few shades darker.

Besides the veg listed here, try tomatoes, corn, mushrooms, shallots, green beans, garlic, garlic scapes, zucchini, purple cabbage, asparagus and even cauliflower. And don't forget aromatics like peppercorns, mustard seeds, and garlic and herbs like dill and thyme. So, go crazy and start pickling!

Add the vegetables and any herbs and spices to a lidded jar, leaving about ½ inch (1.3 cm) of room at the top.

To make the pickling brine, whisk together the vinegar(s), water, sugar and salt.

Pour the brine over the vegetables. Cover tightly, shake around, and let it sit on the counter for 24 hours, shaking occasionally, and then place it in the refrigerator.

The pickles will be ready to eat as soon as the next day but will continue to pickle over time, different vegetables at different rates, so keep an eye on them and be sure to eat them when they are as zesty and tender as you like!

HOW TO MAKE VINAIGRETTE

You can't have a good salad without a good vinaigrette and, just like with pickles, it's all about the ratio. I know there is a traditional French recipe, but it's so heavy on the oil side, the vinegar gets lost. I love the acidic punch that vinegar brings to the table, so I call for equal parts vinegar and oil. Try one, two or all three of the recipes listed here, plus a few more scattered throughout this book, and then use the ratio to experiment with your favorite vinegars!

To make the sherry-shallot vinaigrette, add the shallots to a lidded jar or to a dressing bottle. Cover with the vinegar and let sit for 15 minutes to macerate. Add the olive oil, thyme, lemon zest and salt. Cover and shake well to combine.

To make the white balsamic vinaigrette, add the garlic to a lidded jar or to a dressing bottle. Cover with the vinegar and let sit for 15 minutes to macerate. Add the olive oil, maple syrup, mustard and salt. Cover and shake well to combine.

To make the red wine vinaigrette, add the garlic to a lidded jar or to a dressing bottle. Cover with the vinegar and let sit for 15 minutes to macerate. Add the olive oil, oregano and salt. Cover and shake well to combine.

Vinaigrettes separate, so shake again before using. Store at room temperature.

Makes 1 cup (240 ml) each

SHERRY-SHALLOT VINAIGRETTE

1 tbsp (10 g) finely minced shallots

¼ cup (60 ml) sherry vinegar

¼ cup (60 ml) good olive oil

1 tsp fresh thyme leaves

1 tsp lemon zest

Pinch of salt

WHITE BALSAMIC VINAIGRETTE

1 clove garlic, pressed

¼ cup (60 ml) white balsamic vinegar

¼ cup (60 ml) good olive oil

2 tsp (10 ml) maple syrup

1 tsp grainy mustard

Pinch of salt

RED WINE VINAIGRETTE

1 clove garlic, pressed

¼ cup (60 ml) red wine vinegar

¼ cup (60 ml) good olive oil

¼ tsp dried oregano

Pinch of salt

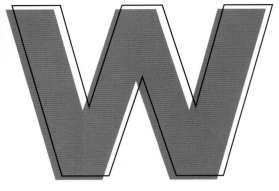

WHOLE GRAINS

W is for whole grains, an essential part of a well-balanced diet. Whole grains are packed with protein, fiber, vitamins, minerals and antioxidants. They have been shown to support healthy digestion, reduce chronic inflammation and lower the risk of diabetes and heart disease. Why wouldn't you want to eat them?

Barley is used to make beer and is also really good to eat. It's a little brown grain that is kind of chewy like brown rice, but with a slightly nutty flavor. It's rich in vitamins and minerals like manganese, selenium, copper, B vitamins, phosphorus and niacin. Like oats, barley is a source of beta-glucan, which has been shown to help to lower cholesterol levels. And it's high in lignans, a group of antioxidants that are linked to a lower risk of cancer and heart disease.

When you are out shopping for barley, you will likely see labels that say hulled, hull-less and pearl. Hulled and hull-less barley are considered to be the whole-grain form; however, hull-less barley has slightly less fiber. Pearl barley is not considered a whole grain because it's processed to remove the outer hull and polished to remove the bran layer. So, go for the whole-grain options.

Barley is relatively neutral. To up the flavor profile, cook it with vegetable broth, vegan butter and bay leaves. Then serve it on top of Balsamic Tempeh Dragon Bowls (page 139) or make Barley with Mushrooms and Dill (page 159).

Millet is a tiny, round, yellow whole grain that is probably most famous as birdseed, but it has been a food crop for human consumption for thousands of years and it's so, so good! It's full of protein and rich in calcium, copper, magnesium and potassium and in essential vitamins like B6, C, E and K. It's also very high in fiber, which supports heart health and good digestion.

When millet cooks, it quadruples in size and you end up with a pot full of fluffy grains. It has a slightly nutty flavor but is also sweet, kind of like corn. And it's naturally gluten-free, which makes it a good sub in recipes that call for grains like barley and bulgur, another healthy whole grain. Make the colorful Millet-Corn Salad with Baby Kale and Garlic-Chive Vinaigrette (page 160), which will become your go-to potluck salad for sure.

Buckwheat is one of the world's first domesticated crops, but its name is deceiving. Buckwheat is not wheat, even though wheat is right there in its name, which apparently comes from the Dutch, *boekweit*, which means beech wheat because the seeds, or groats, resemble the seeds of the beech tree. Anyway, it's not wheat. It's actually a fruit that is classified as a whole grain. And it's gluten-free. Got it?!

Buckwheat is a complete protein, meaning that it contains all nine essential amino acids, another excellent plant-based protein source. It's also high in fiber and rich in iron, phosphorus, manganese, magnesium, copper and zinc, all of which support the immune system.

Buckwheat cooks up chewy and tastes earthy and nutty at the same time. It's the main ingredient in Buckwheat and Bow Ties (page 163).

Buckwheat is also milled into flour and made into noodles, called soba, which is Japanese for buckwheat. They are a staple in Japanese cuisine and can be served hot or cold. And, as you might guess, they taste earthy and nutty. Soba noodles are best when paired with clean and simple sauces, like the one for Cold Sesame Noodles (page 145).

Get to know these whole grains well and find ways to eat them often, even if these are the only recipes you use. They can all be made ahead of time and stored in an airtight container in the refrigerator for up to 1 week or in the freezer for up to 6 months.

BARLEY WITH MUSHROOMS AND DILL

When I was growing up, the only time I ever ate barley was at the deli, in the form of mushroom barley soup. The soup was flavorful, but the barley was always so overcooked. As an adult, I rediscovered barley and realized it's better to make it on its own first and then add stuff to it. That way it can be flavored with vegetable broth and cooked to just the right tenderness. Mixed with onions, carrots, mushrooms and lots of fresh dill, it's like that old mushroom barley soup, but better.

Add the barley, bay leaf, butter and vegetable broth to a pot. Bring to a boil, reduce to a simmer, cover and cook until the barley is tender and soft but still slightly chewy, anywhere from 30 to 45 minutes.

Turn off the heat, remove the bay leaf and let the barley sit covered, for at least 10 minutes. When ready to use, fluff with a fork.

In the meantime, prepare the mushrooms. Heat a pan with sides over medium heat. Add the olive oil. When it's shimmering, add the onions and carrots. Cook until the vegetables start to soften, about 5 minutes. Add the garlic. Mix around and cook until the garlic is fragrant, about 1 minute. Add the mushrooms. Stir them into the vegetables and cook, until the mushrooms start to turn golden brown, about 7 minutes. Season with salt and pepper.

Add the barley to a big mixing bowl. Add the mushroom mixture and mix well.

Top with dill and serve warm or at room temperature.

Serves 4 to 6

BARLEY

1 cup (200 g) uncooked barley

1 bay leaf

1 tbsp (14 g) vegan butter

3 cups (720 ml) vegetable broth

MUSHROOMS

1 tbsp (15 ml) good olive oil

1 onion, thinly sliced into quarter moons

1 carrot, cut into rounds

1 clove garlic, pressed

8 oz (227 g) baby bella mushrooms, thinly sliced

Pinch of salt

Dash of pepper

TO SERVE

Fresh dill, chopped

Serves 4 to 6

MILLET

1 cup (200 g) uncooked millet

Pinch of salt

2 cups (480 ml) water

VEGETABLES

1 tbsp (15 ml) sunflower oil

1 small white onion, finely diced

1 carrot, shredded

1 clove garlic, pressed

½ tsp Aleppo pepper

Pinch of salt

Dash of pepper

2 cups (56 g) baby kale

1½ cups (231 g) sweet corn

GARLIC-CHIVE VINAIGRETTE

1 clove garlic, pressed

¼ cup (60 ml) white balsamic vinegar

¼ cup (60 ml) good olive oil

2 tbsp (6 g) chopped fresh chives

Pinch of salt

TO SERVE

Fresh parsley, chopped

MILLET-CORN SALAD WITH BABY KALE AND GARLIC-CHIVE VINAIGRETTE

Millet is wonderfully nutritious and delicious on its own. It's even better when served with sweet corn, baby kale and tossed in a garlic-chive vinaigrette. If, for some reason, it all doesn't disappear the first go-around, reheat it in a hot skillet with some oil. Don't move it around too much and let the bottom layer crisp up. The millet caramelizes and you end up with little crunchy nuggets of deliciousness.

To prepare the millet, heat a pan with sides over medium heat. Add the millet and stir it around with a wooden spoon. Toast until the millet is fragrant and starts to pop and turn golden brown, about 4 to 5 minutes. Season with salt.

Stand to the side and add the water. Be careful; it will sputter. Bring to a boil, reduce to a simmer, cover and cook until the water is absorbed, about 12 to 15 minutes. Turn off the heat and let the millet sit covered, for at least 10 minutes. When ready to use, fluff with a fork.

In the meantime, prepare the vegetables. Heat a cast-iron or nonstick skillet over medium heat. Add the sunflower oil. When it's shimmering, add the onions and carrots, and cook until the vegetables start to soften, about 5 minutes.

Add the garlic, Aleppo pepper, salt and a dash of pepper; mix around and cook until the garlic is fragrant, about 1 minute. Add the kale and corn and cook until the kale is bright green and the corn is heated through, another 1 or 2 minutes.

To make the vinaigrette, add the garlic to a lidded jar or to a dressing bottle. Cover with the white balsamic vinegar and let it sit for 15 minutes to macerate. Add the olive oil, chives and salt. Cover and shake well to combine.

Add the millet to a big mixing bowl. Add the vegetables and as much vinaigrette as you like and toss to coat.

Top with parsley and serve warm or at room temperature.

BUCKWHEAT AND BOW TIES

I'm calling this recipe buckwheat and bow ties, but it's really kasha varnishkes, a traditional Ashkenazi Jewish dish that was brought to America by Eastern European Jews, like my grandparents. Kasha is toasted buckwheat groats and *varnishkes* is Yiddish for bow-tie-shaped noodles.

There are a few elements to this dish: sweet, silky caramelized onions, toasted buckwheat and, of course, the bow ties. Everything is made separately, which means it could all be done ahead of time. In fact, caramelized onions can be stored in an airtight container in the refrigerator for up to 1 week and in the freezer for up to 6 months! And, if one day you are not into the varnishkes part, just make the kasha and onions part and serve it on its own.

To prepare the onions, heat a pan with sides over medium-low heat. Add the olive oil. When it's shimmering, add the onions. Use tongs to mix the onions around and coat them with the oil. Cover the pan and sweat the onions, until they become translucent and start to soften, about 8 minutes.

Uncover and continue to cook over medium-low heat, stirring occasionally, until the onions are golden and buttery, about 20 to 25 minutes. If the onions start to stick to the pan, add a little bit of water. Take it off the heat and set aside.

To prepare the buckwheat, heat another pan with sides over medium heat. Add the olive oil. When it's shimmering, add the groats. Use a wooden spoon to stir the groats into the oil to coat all of the grains. Toast until the groats smell nutty and turn slightly darker, about 3 minutes. Season with salt.

Hold the lid over the pot so that you are blocking yourself and pour in the boiling water. Be careful; the water will sputter. Reduce the heat to low, cover and cook until all the water is absorbed, about 15 minutes. Turn off the heat and let the groats sit covered, for at least 10 minutes. When ready to use, fluff with a fork.

To make the bow ties, bring a big pot of salted water to a boil and cook the bow ties according to the package instructions. Drain the bow ties and put them back into the pot.

Add the onions and groats to the bow ties and mix well.

Season with a drizzle of olive oil and freshly ground black pepper and serve warm or at room temperature.

Serves 4 to 6

CARAMELIZED ONIONS

1 tsp good olive oil

2 sweet white onions, thinly sliced into half-moons

BUCKWHEAT

1 tbsp (15 ml) good olive oil

1 cup (180 g) uncooked buckwheat groats

Pinch of salt

2 cups (480 ml) boiling water

BOW TIES

½ lb (226 g) uncooked bow ties

TO SERVE

Drizzle of good olive oil

Freshly ground black pepper

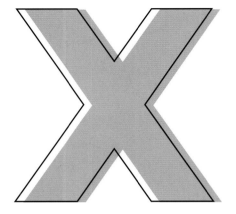

XO SAUCE

There are no ingredients that start with X, but I had to have something for every letter of the alphabet, so when I remembered XO Sauce from a trip I took to Hong Kong (China) in 2003, way back before I was vegan, I knew I had to make a kick-ass version worthy of the name.

The chef at the Peninsula Hotel in Kowloon created a sauce made with expensive ingredients like dried shrimps, dried scallops and aged ham. He called it XO Sauce, as in extra-old aged cognac, because in Hong Kong (China), XO is slang for anything high quality and luxurious. Funny, though, there is no cognac and it's not really a sauce. It's more like a jam or a relish.

According to the chef, XO Sauce is a condiment that should complement a dish, not overpower it. It's supposed to be a rich, intensely salty, slightly sweet sauce with an umami depth to it. Got it. I can do that.

In my version, dried shiitake mushrooms are reconstituted and cooked down with shallots and garlic, then flavored with a combination of tamari, maple syrup, Aleppo pepper, cinnamon and cumin. The result? A rich, intensely salty, slightly sweet sauce!

This unique XO Sauce can take any dish to a whole new level. All you need is a tablespoon or two (or three!). You will see how delicious it is when you make Green Beans and Baby Kale with XO Sauce (page 168) and XO Fried Rice (page 171).

And then use it whenever you want to add flavor. Toss it with noodles, spread it on top of baked tofu, mix it into a tofu scramble or add it to ramen broth. See where I am going with this? The possibilities are endless.

XO SAUCE

Here it is: XO Sauce in all of its vegan glory. Meaty, smoky, earthy, umami-rich dried shiitake mushrooms stand in for all of the expensive ingredients from the original sauce. Sautéed shallots and garlic are seasoned to create layers of flavor—tamari for even more umami, maple syrup for sweetness, Aleppo pepper for fruity heat, and cinnamon and cumin for warmth. The result is a deeply flavorful umami bomb that you can use a million different ways.

Place the dried shiitakes in a heatproof bowl. Pour just enough boiling water over the mushrooms to cover them. Let them sit to rehydrate, about 15 minutes.

In the meantime, heat a pan with sides over low heat. Add the sunflower oil. When it's shimmering, add the shallots and garlic. Cook until the shallots start to soften and become translucent and the garlic is fragrant, about 8 minutes.

Add the tamari, maple syrup, Aleppo pepper, cumin and cinnamon stick or ground cinnamon. Stir into the shallots. Continue to cook until the liquid is absorbed, another few minutes.

Lift the shiitakes out of the soaking liquid, squeezing them as you go. Remove the stems and coarsely chop the caps. Add them to the pan and stir into the shallots.

Strain the soaking liquid through a paper towel. Pour ½ cup (120 ml) into the mushroom-shallot mixture and reserve the rest. Cook until the liquid is absorbed, about a minute.

Turn off the heat and let the mushroom-shallot mixture stand to cool. Once cooled, remove the cinnamon stick (if using) and transfer the mixture to the bowl of a small food processor. Pulse a few times, until the mixture is chopped. Remove about ½ cup (113 g) and set aside. Add 1 tablespoon (15 ml) of the reserved soaking liquid and puree the mixture until it is as smooth as you can get it. Turn it out into the reserved mixture and mix to combine.

Store in an airtight container in the refrigerator for up to 2 weeks or in the freezer for up to 6 months.

Makes approximately
1 cup (240 ml)

1 oz (28 g) dried shiitake mushrooms

Boiling water

1 tbsp (15 ml) sunflower oil

4 shallots, thinly sliced

3 big cloves garlic, pressed

1 tbsp (15 ml) tamari

1 tbsp (15 ml) maple syrup

1 tbsp (6 g) Aleppo pepper

½ tsp cumin

1 cinnamon stick or ¼ tsp ground cinnamon

½ cup (120 ml) plus 1 tbsp (15 ml) strained mushroom soaking liquid, divided

Serves 4

1 lb (454 g) green beans, trimmed and sliced into 1-inch (2.5-cm) pieces

½ cup (120 ml) water

1 tbsp (14 g) vegan butter

Pinch of salt

3 cups (84 g) baby kale

¼ cup (60 ml) XO Sauce (page 167)

GREEN BEANS AND BABY KALE WITH XO SAUCE

Green beans don't have to be boring. XO them up! Steam them with a little butter, toss them with baby kale and season them with a lot of XO Sauce. You end up with a really exciting, umami-rich side dish that serves a crowd. But you don't have to wait for everyone else. Cut down the measurements and make enough just for yourself!

Heat a lidded wide shallow pan over medium heat. When it's hot, add the green beans, water, butter and salt. Cover and steam for 5 to 8 minutes, until the green beans turn bright green.

Remove the lid, add the kale and use tongs to toss it around until it's completely wilted, about 1 minute. Turn off the heat and stir in the XO Sauce.

Serve warm or at room temperature.

XO FRIED RICE

Old, cold, frozen rice is the secret to excellent fried rice. That's because just-cooked rice is too new. It will be sticky and soft, and your fried rice will come out wet, gummy and mushy. So, next time you prepare plain rice for dinner, make extra and store it in an airtight container in the refrigerator for up to 1 week or in the freezer for up to 6 months.

When you want to make fried rice, hit up your stash. If the rice is frozen, take it out of the freezer and defrost it in the refrigerator the night before. Take it out a little bit before you are ready to cook, sauté up any vegetables you have on hand—I always have scallions, carrots, zucchini and frozen peas, but literally anything goes—and season it with XO Sauce. The whole thing takes about 10 minutes from start to finish and you end up with one of the easiest and most delicious meals ever.

1 tbsp (15 ml) sunflower oil

2 scallions, white and green parts, thinly sliced

1 carrot, shredded

1 small zucchini, diced

1 tbsp (15 ml) tamari, or more to taste

2 cups (372 g) cold cooked rice

½ cup (67 g) frozen peas

¼ cup (60 ml) XO Sauce (page 167)

TO SERVE

1 scallion, white and green parts, thinly sliced

2 tsp (4 g) toasted sesame seeds

Heat a cast-iron or nonstick skillet over medium-low heat. Add the sunflower oil. When it's shimmering, add the scallions, carrots and zucchini. Season with tamari. Cook until the vegetables soften, about 3 to 5 minutes.

Add the rice, peas and XO Sauce. Use a wooden spoon to mix everything together. Cook, stirring occasionally, until the rice is heated through, about 5 to 7 minutes.

Serve topped with scallions and toasted sesame seeds.

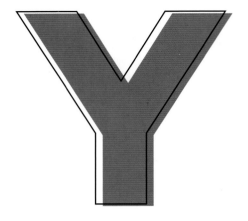

YOGURT

Move over, dairy yogurt, there is a new game in town! That's right. It's dairy-free, vegan, plant-based, eco-friendly, creamy, really good and getting better every day. It's made from every plant-based milk you can think of—coconut, cashew, almond, oat and soy—as well as pea protein, cassava root and pili nuts.

Yogurt is really healthy. It's rich in protein, fiber and vitamins. And, live active cultures are good for gut health and good digestion.

Dairy-free yogurt has come a long way in the last decade, with both new and classic brands releasing new products all the time. Like anything else that has flooded the market, there is a wide range in terms of quality, flavor and texture. Yogurt should be smooth and creamy (not gritty or runny), with a delightfully tangy yogurt flavor.

The best yogurts have few ingredients. Just the plant-milk base, live and active cultures, and maybe a natural thickening agent. There should be nothing weird, no unrecognizable or unpronounceable ingredients, and if there are no active cultures, it's not yogurt. Always be sure to check that the label is marked with a vegan certification, because some so-called plant-based yogurt brands still add dairy and other animal products, for some bizarre reason.

In this book, no matter the recipe, I call for plain, unsweetened yogurt. It's the most versatile and the healthiest option, plus you can sweeten it yourself, if need be, with coconut sugar or maple syrup. Again, check the label, because even some unsweetened brands still add sugar, for some other bizarre reason.

Once you find your favorite brand, enjoy it simply topped with The Only Granola Recipe You'll Ever Need (page 109) or as the base for Tzatziki Sauce (page 176).

Yogurt can be used as more than a condiment. It's the key ingredient in what is sure to become your new favorite thing, Yogurt Flatbread (page 175). Yogurt adds creaminess to Modern Portobello Stroganoff (page 115) and adds just the right tang in this gorgeous Banana-Caramel Upside-Down Cake (page 45).

YOGURT FLATBREAD

Makes 4

These flatbreads come together so fast, you better be ready to eat! In less than 10 minutes, you will have warm, fresh bread, bread that has all the tang of sourdough without the starter and all the kneading. The secret ingredient? Yogurt! It does everything that needs to happen to make bread with a crispy exterior and a chewy interior. Be sure to add yogurt to your weekly shopping list so you can make these flatbreads anytime!

1 cup (125 g) all-purpose flour, plus more for dusting

1 tsp baking powder

½ tsp baking soda

½ tsp salt

⅔ cup (160 ml) plain unsweetened vegan yogurt

Olive oil, for cooking

Add the flour, baking powder, baking soda and salt to a big mixing bowl. Whisk together.

Add the yogurt. Use a silicone spatula to combine into a shaggy dough. It will be sticky, so dust it with a bit of flour as you work the dough into a smooth ball.

Use a bench scraper to cut the dough into 4 pieces. Roll each one into a little ball.

Heat a dry cast-iron griddle or nonstick pan over medium heat.

Working one at a time, drizzle a little bit of olive oil over the dough ball to coat it. Use your fingers to flatten it out and finesse it into a circle or an oval, about ⅛ inch (3 mm) thick. There is no right or wrong shape!

Place the flatbread on the hot griddle or pan. Cook the first side until the top looks bubbly, dry and a little puffy, about 30 seconds to 1 minute. Flip and cook the other side, for another 30 seconds. Repeat until all the flatbreads are cooked.

Serves 4

TEMPEH GYROS WITH TZATZIKI SAUCE

This might look like a long list of ingredients, but after a little marinating, chopping and mixing, you've got a really impressive Greek-inspired meal that comes together in the time it takes to bake the tempeh. Be sure you pick your favorite yogurt for this one, because the tzatziki sauce is the most important part of the dish—creamy, herby, tangy and full of flavor.

TEMPEH

1 (8-oz [227-g]) package soy tempeh, thinly sliced the short way, about 24 pieces

2 tbsp (30 ml) good olive oil

2 tbsp (30 ml) fresh lemon juice

2 tbsp (30 ml) tamari

1 tsp garlic powder

1 tsp dried oregano

½ tsp onion powder

Dash of pepper

TZATZIKI SAUCE

1 clove garlic, pressed

1 tbsp (15 ml) fresh lemon juice

1 (5.3-oz [150-ml]) container plain unsweetened vegan yogurt

1 Persian cucumber, diced

1 tbsp (3 g) chopped fresh dill

1 tsp chopped fresh mint

1 tsp lemon zest

Pinch of salt

SALAD

1 head romaine lettuce, shredded

4 tomatoes, cut into slices or quarters

½ small red onion, thinly sliced into half-moons

2 tbsp (7 g) chopped fresh dill

Red Wine Vinaigrette (page 155)

TO SERVE

Yogurt Flatbread (page 175)

Place the tempeh in a pot and cover with water. Bring to a boil, reduce to a simmer and cook, uncovered, for 10 minutes.

Preheat the oven to 350°F (177°C). Line a half sheet pan with parchment paper.

In a medium mixing bowl, whisk together the olive oil, lemon juice, tamari, garlic powder, oregano, onion powder and pepper.

When the tempeh has finished simmering, drain it and drop it into the marinade, flipping it over to coat both sides. Place the tempeh on the sheet pan. Pour any extra marinade over the top of the tempeh. Bake for 25 to 30 minutes, until the tempeh is crispy around the edges.

In the meantime, make the tzatziki sauce. Add the garlic and lemon juice to a small mixing bowl. Let it sit for 15 minutes to macerate. Add the yogurt, cucumbers, dill, mint, lemon zest and salt. Mix to combine.

To make the salad, add the romaine, tomatoes, onions and dill to a big mixing bowl. Add as much vinaigrette as you like and toss to coat.

Serve the tempeh, tzatziki sauce, salad and flatbreads buffet style so everyone can assemble their own gyro.

ZUCCHINI

What else could the letter Z possibly be other than zucchini? It's one of the most abundant and versatile ingredients and also there is no other vegetable that starts with Z.

Zucchini is a super-healthy ingredient, rich in beneficial plant compounds like vitamins A and B, iron, calcium and zinc. Zucchini has more potassium than a banana, which helps to lower blood pressure, lowering the risk of stroke and heart disease. It's high in fiber, which is good for digestion, and rich in antioxidants like manganese, which benefit skin and eye health.

Zucchini is a member of the summer squash family, which means it's harvested while the skin is still soft, compared to winter squashes like acorn and pumpkin. Zucchini is indigenous to the Americas, but fast-forward a few thousand years to the variety we eat today. The long, speckled green zucchini we know and love was cultivated in Italy in the 19th century, which is where the name comes from. Zucchini means "little squash" in Italian!

Zucchini is mild in flavor with tender flesh and edible skin and seeds. Zucchini are cylindrical, with round bottoms and straight necks, which is what distinguishes them from other summer squashes. Those have crooked and/or tapered necks and firmer flesh. Besides the classic green speckled zucchini, you might also find bright yellow golden ones and green-and-white striped ones. They taste pretty much the same as green zucchini but add extra color to your creations.

You might also see fun, fat little round green zucchini, known as eight balls, which tastes just like regular zucchini but is ideal for stuffing. If you are into that kind of thing, cut the top off, use a spoon to dig out the insides and, boom, you have a decorative edible vehicle for Zesty Quinoa Pilaf (page 122) or Millet-Corn Salad with Baby Kale and Garlic-Chive Vinaigrette (page 160).

When you are out shopping for zucchini, look for ones that are firm (not mushy or bendy) with shiny, healthy skin. You want zucchini that are around six to eight inches (15 to 20 cm) long, the point at which they are perfectly tender and the seeds are still small. The bigger they get, the tougher the skin, the more fibrous the flesh and the bigger the seeds. They are still good, just more seedy than fleshy.

Zucchini is super versatile and available all year round. It can be eaten raw or cooked and prepared in a myriad of ways—spiralized, peeled, shredded, baked, grilled and sautéed. My favorite way to showcase raw zucchini is to thinly slice it and serve it as carpaccio, as in Zucchini Carpaccio with Fresh Herbs and Umeboshi Vinaigrette (page 181). If you have a spiralizer, you can make zucchini noodles, affectionately known as zoodles, and toss them with sauce and pretend they are pasta!

No matter what you do with zucchini, you really can't go wrong. It's a great addition to XO Fried Rice (page 171), Zesty Quinoa Pilaf (page 122) and this unique Green Minestrone (page 182). It adds color and flavor to Caponata with Dates and Two Vinegars (page 32) and an extra boost of nutrition to these Lasagna Rolls with Tofu Ricotta (page 140). And finally, and maybe my all-time favorite way to eat zucchini, Zucchini-Dill Pancakes with Lemon-Chive Aioli (page 185).

One more thing: If you happen to be at the farmers market in the summertime, keep an eye out for zucchini blossoms, the bright yellow-orange flowers that produce zucchini. They are an ingredient in their own right and fun to try at least once. They are delicate and pretty and taste like the essence of zucchini. Stuff them with Tofu Ricotta (page 140) and pan-fry them, add them to a salad or a tofu scramble or decorate a vegan pizza with them.

ZUCCHINI CARPACCIO WITH FRESH HERBS AND UMEBOSHI VINAIGRETTE

Raw zucchini is like a blank canvas. It has a kind of fresh-out-of-the-garden mild flavor that can be taken in any direction. In this pretty salad, long, thin slices of zucchini are tossed with fresh herbs and peppery radishes and drizzled with tangy umeboshi vinaigrette. The vinegar not only flavors the zucchini, but it changes the texture dramatically. You can dress this salad right before you serve it or let it sit overnight. The longer it sits, the softer the zucchini becomes, so have fun with the texture and see at what point you like it best!

To prepare the carpaccio, add the zucchini ribbons, radishes, lemon zest, basil, chives and mint to a big mixing bowl. Toss gently to combine.

To make the vinaigrette, add the white balsamic vinegar, olive oil, umeboshi paste, maple syrup and salt to a lidded jar or to a dressing bottle. Cover and shake well to combine.

Arrange the carpaccio on a platter in a pleasing way and drizzle with as much vinaigrette as you like.

Served topped with Seedy Sprinkle Cheese.

CARPACCIO

2 big zucchinis, peeled into ribbons with a vegetable peeler

2 radishes, thinly sliced on a mandoline

1 tsp lemon zest

1 tbsp (3 g) chopped fresh basil

1 tbsp (3 g) chopped fresh chives

1 tbsp (6 g) chopped fresh mint

UMEBOSHI VINAIGRETTE

1 tbsp (15 ml) white balsamic vinegar

1 tbsp (15 ml) good olive oil

1 tbsp (18 g) umeboshi paste

1 tsp maple syrup

Pinch of salt

TO SERVE

Seedy Sprinkle Cheese (page 79)

Serves 4

1 tbsp (15 ml) good olive oil

1 leek, white and light green parts, cleaned and cut into rounds

1 carrot, cut into rounds

1 rib celery, cut into half-moons

1 clove garlic, pressed

Pinch of salt

Dash of pepper

1 medium-sized zucchini, cut into half-moons

1½ cups (246 g) cooked or 1 (15-oz [425-g]) can garbanzo beans, drained

3 cups (720 ml) water

1 cup (134 g) frozen peas

¼ lb (113 g) uncooked ditalini or other small pasta

TO SERVE

Fresh parsley, chopped

Lemon zest

GREEN MINESTRONE

A no-tomato minestrone? Yes! A favorite of my testers, this recipe is packed with half-moons of zucchini and bright green vegetables. It can be made all year round, but it may become your go-to during zucchini season. Garbanzo beans add an extra protein punch and fresh herbs brighten it up. And don't forget the zest! The fresh hit of lemon brightens the whole bowl.

Heat a heavy-bottomed soup pot over medium heat. Add the olive oil. When it's shimmering, add the leeks, carrots and celery and cook until translucent, about 5 minutes. Add the garlic, salt and pepper, and mix around and cook until the garlic is fragrant, about 1 minute.

Add the zucchini, garbanzo beans and water. Bring to a boil, reduce to a simmer and cook with the cover askew until the zucchini is tender, about 8 to 10 minutes. Add the peas and cook for another minute or so, until the peas are heated through.

In the meantime, make the ditalini. Bring a big pot of salted water to a boil and cook according to the package instructions. Drain and add the ditalini to the soup and mix well.

Serve topped with parsley and lemon zest.

WHERE DO YOU GET YOUR PROTEIN?

If you tell people you bought a vegan cookbook, they will instantly become worried about your protein intake. It's probably the number one question I get and here is the answer: everywhere. In fact, six of our star ingredients are complete proteins—buckwheat, hemp seeds, nutritional yeast, quinoa, tempeh and tofu—and there is protein in almost every other ingredient in this book. So, tell everyone not to worry. If elephants and hippos and gorillas and cows can get enough protein on a plant-based diet, so can you!

ZUCCHINI-DILL PANCAKES WITH LEMON-CHIVE AIOLI

I love any food in the form of pancakes, and these zucchini pancakes are no exception. They are super easy to make—just zucchini, dill and some garbanzo bean flour. They come out crispy on the outside and tender on the inside. They are so, so good right out of the skillet, but they are even better dipped in lemony aioli for some extra flavor and freshness.

I'm just warning you now. You might have to make a double batch, because, if you are anything like me, half of them won't even make it out of the kitchen.

Place the shredded zucchini into a fine-mesh sieve over a bowl. Sprinkle with 1 teaspoon of salt and mix around with a fork. Let the zucchini stand to drain, about 10 minutes. Use the fork to press the zucchini against the sieve to release as much water as possible. Set aside.

To make the flax egg, whisk together the ground flaxseed and water in a small mixing bowl. Set aside for 5 minutes to thicken.

Add the garbanzo bean flour and baking powder to a medium mixing bowl. Whisk to combine. Add the flax egg, zucchini, dill and scallions. Mix until a batter forms.

Line a quarter sheet pan with paper towels.

Heat a cast-iron or nonstick skillet over medium heat. Add the sunflower oil. When it's shimmering, it's time to cook the pancakes. Scoop up a heaping table-spoon (15 g) of the mixture and drop it gently onto the oil, pressing the top down ever so slightly.

Cook 3 to 4 pancakes at a time, without crowding the pan, until the bottom sides are golden brown, about 5 minutes. Carefully flip them over, flattening them just a bit with a spatula and cook until the new bottom sides are golden brown.

Place the pancakes onto the paper towels to absorb the excess oil. Add more oil to the pan and continue to make pancakes until all of the batter is gone.

To make the aioli, add the mayo, garlic, chives, lemon zest, lemon juice and salt to a small mixing bowl. Mix together and place in a dipping bowl.

Serve warm or at room temperature with aioli on the side.

ZUCCHINI

1 big zucchini, shredded

1 tsp salt

FLAX EGG

1 tbsp (10 g) ground flaxseed

3 tbsp (45 ml) water

PANCAKES

¼ cup (30 g) garbanzo bean flour

½ tsp baking powder

¼ cup (13 g) chopped fresh dill

2 scallions, white and green parts, thinly sliced

Sunflower oil, for cooking

LEMON-CHIVE AIOLI

¼ cup (60 ml) Five-Minute Mayo (page 15)

1 clove garlic, pressed

2 tbsp (6 g) minced fresh chives

1 tbsp (6 g) lemon zest

½ tbsp (8 ml) fresh lemon juice

Pinch of salt

RECIPES BY CATEGORY

ACKNOWLEDGMENTS

Thank you so much to Will Kiester for giving me another opportunity to do what I love—writing cookbooks! Thank you to Marissa Giambelluca for working with me to create the best alphabetical list of ingredients. You said to get creative, so I gave you XO Sauce! Thank you to Meg Baskis for designing such a pretty book. Thank you to Maude Campbell for painstakingly working through the copy with me to make it as perfect as it could possibly be and for the metric conversions. And thank you to everyone else at Page Street Publishing who worked to bring this book to life.

Thank you to Alex Shytsman for once again turning my living room into a set, making everything look perfect and for doing it all while wearing a mask. Can't wait to collaborate again!

Thank you to Benay Vynerib for enthusiastically picking up food five nights in a row. I told you I would cook for you, so I made you my whole book!

Thank you to Aleen LaPrelle and Jessica Soul. Between the both of you, you made every single recipe in this book. I am honored that you spent your time and money to test these recipes, check my work and make suggestions. If you look carefully, you will see your comments and ideas incorporated into the text. Thank you also to Nicole Benson and Carla Slajchert.

Thank you to Chef Allison Kennedy, Bob Roth, Dianne Wenz, Erica Kubersky and everyone at Orchard Grocer, Dr. Ethan Ciment, Hannah Kaminsky, Jenn Sebestyen, Joey Arbagey, Linda Soper-Kolton, Nava Atlas, Dr. Neal Barnard and Peta Leith for all of your kind words and support.

Thank you to everyone who subscribes to and shares my blog. It's been ten years and I'm still going! Thank you to everyone who bought my first book, *Wait, That's Vegan?!*, and to everyone who visits me on Instagram. Thank you for making my recipes and asking for more!

Thank you to my parents, Diana and Jerry, for your never-ending encouragement and support. Thank you to my sister Debbie and my nephew Jonah for your endless cheerleading. Thank you to my friend Robin Finn for thirty-plus years of friendship and wise words right when I need them.

Thank you to my son, Luke. Your taste tests, feedback and brilliant ideas were instrumental in the creation of the recipes in this book. And thank you for being the tiebreaker! Thank you to my husband, Paul. You always go above and beyond. Shopping by FaceTime is my new favorite thing.

Thank you to my friends at A Matter of Health. You showed up so we could have fresh food on our table.

Thank you to all of the essential workers who worked hard to keep us safe here in New York City during the global pandemic of 2020. I started writing this book within days of the lockdown when food was scarce, there were lines around the corner and we applauded the essential workers every night at 7 p.m. For you, I am donating a portion of what I earn for writing this book to Heal the Healers Now, a division of the David Lynch Foundation, which provides free Transcendental Meditation training to those working on the front lines.

ABOUT THE AUTHOR

Lisa Dawn Angerame lives in New York City with her husband and son. A longtime vegan, she is the author of *Wait, That's Vegan?!* and the creator of Lisa's Project: Vegan, a blog chronicling her vegan cooking adventures. Lisa Dawn holds a certificate in Plant-Based Nutrition from eCornell and graduated from the Rouxbe Online Culinary School, rouxbe.com, as a certified Plant-Based Professional and from the Essential Vegan Desserts course. She is committed to expanding awareness about veganism by making delicious food and believes that anyone can learn to love and learn to cook with vegan ingredients.

www.lisasprojectvegan.com

@lisasprojectvegan

INDEX